"For many of us, the idea of having a mentor is appealing, and the suggestion of being a mentor is intimidating. Through this book, Melissa Kruger helps both the mentor and the mentee know where to start, what to cover, and how to make it work so that the mentoring relationship is a source of joy and growth for everyone involved."

Nancy Guthrie, Bible teacher; author, *Even Better than Eden: Nine Ways the Bible's Story Changes Everything about Your Story*

"Mentoring and discipleship are essential for the Christian life, yet so many of us don't quite know how to do it. *Growing Together* is not only needed; it's also exactly the book we've been looking for. Melissa Kruger has written an instructive, biblically grounded, accessible, practical, and versatile book perfect for one-on-one mentoring relationships, groups, or individuals. Women who read this book will grow together in their faith as well as be equipped to do the work of ministry. I'm grateful for this resource and highly recommend it!"

Trillia Newbell, author, *If God Is for Us: The Everlasting Truth of Our Great Salvation*

"*Growing Together* is a resource for mentoring relationships that facilitates meaningful conversations centered around God's word. Engaging questions and simple yet transformative suggestions for application will encourage women to grow together in godliness. This is an invaluable tool for any discipleship tool belt, and I am so thankful to add it to mine!"

Hunter Beless, Founder and Executive Director, *Journeywomen* podcast

Growing Together

Growing Together

*Taking Mentoring beyond Small
Talk and Prayer Requests*

Melissa B. Kruger

WHEATON, ILLINOIS

Trade paperback ISBN: 978-1-4335-6801-5
ePub ISBN: 978-1-4335-6804-6
PDF ISBN: 978-1-4335-6802-2
Mobipocket ISBN: 978-1-4335-6803-9

Library of Congress Cataloging-in-Publication Data

Names: Kruger, Melissa B., author.
Title: Growing together : taking mentoring beyond small talk and prayer requests / Melissa B. Kruger.
Description: Wheaton, Illinois : Crossway, 2020. | Includes bibliographical references.
Identifiers: LCCN 2019032194 (print) | LCCN 2019032195 (ebook) | ISBN 9781433568015 (trade paperback) | ISBN 9781433568022 (pdf) | ISBN 9781433568039 (mobi) | ISBN 9781433568046 (epub)
Subjects: LCSH: Church work with women. | Women in church work. | Mentoring in church work. | Great Commission (Bible)
Classification: LCC BV4445 .K78 2020 (print) | LCC BV4445 (ebook) | DDC 253.082–dc23
LC record available at https://lccn.loc.gov/2019032194
LC ebook record available at https://lccn.loc.gov/2019032195

Crossway is a publishing ministry of Good News Publishers.

BP		31	30	29	28	27	26	25	24	23	22	21
17	16	15	14	13	12	11	10	9	8	7	6	5

For my daughters Emma and Kate,
and my nieces, Elizabeth, Jane Murry, Millie,
Reagan, and Anne Randolph

May there be women in every season who faithfully
invest in you, passing on the truths of the gospel from
one generation to the next. And, may you share what
you've learned with those who follow after you— the
world needs the treasure you've been given.

Contents

Introduction

As women's ministry coordinator at my church, I interact with women in a variety of seasons and stages of life. One of the most frequent requests from younger women is help finding a spiritual mentor. For each lady requesting, there are a variety of hopes behind this longing. Some know they need to grow in their faith and desire an older woman to provide guidance and wisdom. Some long for a nurturing figure to encourage them. Some lack direction and hope that a mentor could give them advice. Some are hurting and hoping for healing as they share their struggles with another. Others feel overwhelmed and are looking for someone who might provide help to ease the burdens of life.

When I approach older women with the request of mentoring, they are often hesitant. Most of them have never been mentored themselves, and they rightly wonder, *What exactly does she want from me?* They may even be fearful, not assured of their ability to lead another because of past personal failure. Some desire to mentor but lack clarity and training on how to do it.

The longing of the younger woman and the hesitancy of the older woman are what have encouraged me to pick up my pen and write. Sometimes it's difficult to know how to move past small talk and go deeper with one another. What I hope to provide is a hands-on tool that a mentor and mentee can use together as a springboard for mentoring discussions. Therefore, this book is not primarily about the concept of mentoring.

Other writers, such as Susan Hunt,[1] have already provided excellent resources for the church on the concept of discipleship. What I hope to offer is a book that women can pick up and use to promote life-giving discussions on a variety of topics that foster and encourage one another's faith. For that reason, this book isn't a book *about* mentoring but rather a book to *use* in the mentoring relationship.

The ultimate goal of this book is for two women to grow together as they walk together. As an older believer shares her wisdom, understanding, and love for the Lord, the younger believer learns from her experience. Mentoring helps give shape to the commands of Scripture. To see an older woman living out gentleness, love, joy, and kindness puts flesh on these words so we can see what they look like in action. The good news about discipleship is that the learning isn't just one way—the older woman grows too! As she recounts God's faithfulness and shares God's word, her own heart is refreshed and revived. Growing together in Christ-centered relationship fosters a more intimate relationship with Jesus for both the younger and older woman.

Structure

This book is arranged with eleven chapters that can be worked through in a variety of ways. You can meet once a month, every other week, or weekly, depending upon your availability. Whatever pace you set, I encourage you to find a day and time that works for you both and schedule your meetings in advance.

The first two chapters briefly explore the concept of mentoring, provide scriptural examples of mentoring, and offer practical considerations about developing a mentor relationship. These two chapters set the foundation for the mentoring relationship so that both participants have similar expectations as they begin.

The next nine chapters provide a curriculum of sorts to help guide you in your time together. Entire books have been written on each of these topics, so these chapters are intended to help start the conversation, not cover the topic fully. Since these are introductory-level chapters, there's an appendix that provides further reading for each topic if you want to dive deeper into one particular subject.

To encourage balanced spiritual growth, these chapters are arranged in a way to help foster a person's relationship with God and the world.

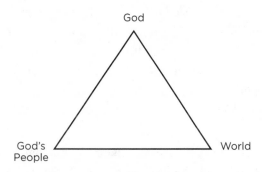

The goal is to cycle through each of these areas on a rotating basis. Topics about our relationship with God (Bible reading, prayer, and contentment) are interspersed with chapters about living in community as believers (church, family, and service), as well as with chapters about our engagement in the world (evangelism, temptations, and discernment). The hope is that balanced discipleship will lead to growth in each of these important areas. Each of these chapters follows a general pattern:

- Wisdom for life: What does the Bible say about a particular topic? Why is it important?
- Wandering in unbelief: Why do we struggle to follow God's teaching in a certain area?
- Walking by faith: How do I live biblical truths in light of the gospel?

At the end of each chapter I'll offer three activities:

- Before you meet: practical tools to help you grow
- While you meet: questions for discussion
- Until you meet again: growing in godliness

These questions and activities are provided to help springboard from the theoretical to the personal. Both the mentor and mentee can answer these questions and engage in the different topics. Even those mature in their faith need to be spurred on in their own spiritual growth. If you're the mentor, don't be afraid to share your own areas of weakness and need for growth. It helps when both people can share openly with each other and support each other. If you're the mentee, I encourage you to listen to, respect, and consider the advice of your mentor. She has wisdom and perspective from years of walking with the Lord and can help you discern what is best.

Wording

Throughout the book I'll use certain terms interchangeably. Mentoring can also be called "discipleship" or "spiritual mothering." When discussing the mentor, I might also use the phrase *older woman*. Please note that the mentor is not necessarily older in physical age. By using the phrase *older woman*, I am speaking about the maturity of her faith, not the length of her years. In turn, I will often use the words *mentee* or *younger woman* to describe the woman being mentored.

These are simply terms to help the reader understand the distinction in the roles. It doesn't mean that the mentee never imparts wisdom to the mentor or that the mentor is an expert in every area of life. Both mentor and mentee are disciples of Jesus, seeking to know him more. One is just further along in the faith, seeking to impart to the other what she has learned.

Different Ways to Use This Book

The primary purpose of this book is one-on-one discipleship. However, it can be used in a few other ways.

Discipleship Groups

Discipleship groups usually consist of one older woman meeting with two to four younger women in the faith. This book can easily be used in this type of setting. Working through certain chapters, such as chapter 2, may require two meetings or a longer meeting time so that everyone will have time to share.

Small-Group Studies

This book can also be used for a small group of ten to twenty women who regularly meet together. To get to know one another over the course of the study, each week one woman from the group could use the guidelines offered in chapter 2 to tell her personal story of faith (rather than attempting to have everyone share the same week). Because of time constraints, it might help to cover the discussion questions first and then have a woman tell her story in the last ten to fifteen minutes of the meeting. I encourage the leaders of the group to share their own story first as an example. The goal of the "Sharing Your Story" exercise is not to tell everything from your past (that might take a little more time than ten minutes!), but to communicate the important moments when God clearly was at work, opening your heart to the message of the gospel.

On Your Own

For many years early in my marriage, my husband and I moved together to different cities. During those times, I desired a mentor but didn't live in one place long enough to establish or seek out that type of relationship. Instead, older women in the faith became my mentors through their books. Elisabeth Elliot, Kay Arthur, Cynthia Heald, Susan Hunt, and many other female authors spurred me on in the faith.

While they weren't physically present, their words became faithful encouragement for my soul. If you are lacking older women in your church or haven't found a woman with whom you can walk this journey, I hope these chapters walk alongside you and encourage your faith. It's an honor for me to pass on to you the truths graciously shared with me by older women of faith.

Years ago I read a poem titled "Call Back," which was first published in the early 1900s.[2] After reading it, I knew I wanted to spend my life "calling back." I'm so thankful for the many women in my own life who have called back and cheered me on in the faith. I hope it will encourage you as we begin.

If you have gone a little way ahead of me, call back—
'Twill cheer my heart and help my feet along the stony track;
And, if perchance, Faith's light is dim, because the oil is low,
Your call will guide my lagging course as wearily I go.

Call back, and tell me that He went with you into the storm;
Call back, and say He kept you when the forest's roots were torn;
That, when the heavens thundered and the earthquake shook
    the hill,
He bore you up and held you when the very air was still.

O friend, call back and tell me, for I cannot see your face;
They say it glows with triumph, and your feet bound in the
    race;
But there are mists between us and my spirit eyes are dim,
And I cannot see the glory, though I long for word of Him.

But if you'll say He heard you when your prayer was but
    a cry,
And if you'll say He saw you through the night's
    sin-darkened sky—
If you have gone a little way ahead, O friend, call back—
'Twill cheer my heart and help my feet along the stony track.

—S. P. W.

Mentoring is a privilege. It is needed. It is a blessing. May you call back to others as you grow together in the faith.

1

We Need One Another

Women need women who will share their lives to train them how to apply the Word to all of life—how to love others, care for their families, cultivate community, work productively, and extend compassion according to God's Word.

—Susan Hunt

In my freshman year of high school, my older brother kept trying to convince me to come with him to FCA (Fellowship of Christian Athletes). While I found it nice that he was actually inviting me to hang out with his friends, I had no desire to go to a big group meeting with him. Eventually, he persuaded me to come, and slowly I became a regular attender at the meetings.

Our FCA advisor was a young unmarried math teacher named Tracey Lafevers. She was energetic and fun as well as discerning and wise. That summer we were invited to share in her wedding day, and I watched with joy as she became Mrs. H. B. Moore.

Thankfully, her new marital status didn't prevent her from continuing as our advisor. Both she and H. B. came to all of our weekly meetings and invested their time and energy into sharing the gospel with students. Over the next three years, I spent hours after school in her classroom planning events and working on Bible studies. We had ski retreats and beach retreats as well as summer fellowship meetings.

By my senior year, I'd often skip going off campus with my friends for lunch and just bring my sandwich up to her room for a chat. Her advice prepared me for life after high school in countless ways. The greatest way she encouraged me through those years was by pointing me to God's word in an effort to grow my faith.

Tracy was my first spiritual mentor. Neither she nor I would have called her that at the time. Our relationship just happened as she chose to invest in the lives of students at the public high school where she taught. She helped me process dating, friendships, and how to live a godly life. She put flesh on the gospel and lived it in front of me so I could learn from her example.

Spiritual mentors are vital for growth. Women ahead of us in the faith can look back and cheer us on in our race. They've been right where we are and often have the scars to prove it. We can learn from them and gain wisdom from their experiences.

We also need to become women who mentor. By God's grace, we have the opportunity to call back to younger believers and spur them on in the faith. As we teach others, the truths of God become more firmly rooted in our own hearts. Both the mentor and the disciple grow in grace as they grow together.

We'll spend this chapter exploring the concept of mentoring—seeking to understand what it means to mentor, what the Bible says about mentoring, and the goal of mentoring. While this book is primarily for a mentor and disciple to use together in the mentoring process, it's helpful to have a basic framework before we begin.

The Meaning of Mentoring

As a little girl, I remember an afternoon I spent playing in the front yard while my Dad was busy picking up sticks and weeding. At one point, he stopped his usual work and went into the garage. He came back with some tools and began doing something I'd never seen him do before. There was a young thin tree that was bent over, suffering from the damaging effects of a storm that had recently blown through. (And, if I remember correctly, it was also suffering from the effects of neighborhood children—myself included—who liked to bounce on its bent-over limb for fun.) He took a rope and tethered the young tree to a much older tree—one that was sturdy and strong, standing straight. When I asked him why he was tying the two trees together, he explained that the older tree could offer support and strength to prevent the younger tree from growing askew. The older tree had withstood years of winds and storms. Just by standing beside the younger tree, it offered stability.

This image comes to mind whenever I think about discipleship. Essentially, the mentoring relationship is one in which a younger woman is tethered to a more mature believer for a season so that she might grow firm in her faith and be equipped for ministry. Just as the older tree doesn't make the younger tree grow (the water and the sun do that), the mentor isn't responsible for the spiritual growth of the mentee (God does that). She's simply standing beside the younger woman, offering the strength she's gained as God has grown her through the years.

Defining Mentoring

With this metaphor in mind, the definition I use for mentoring is this:

> Mentoring is a discipleship relationship that focuses on equipping younger believers for the work of ministry so that they grow in maturity and unity in the faith with the ultimate goal of glorifying God.

We'll begin by considering various Scripture passages to help us unpack this definition, and then we'll explore the relationship between Moses and Joshua as an example to follow.

A Discipleship Relationship

Before Jesus ascended to heaven, he gave his disciples a final command, often called the "Great Commission":

> Jesus came and said to them, "All authority in heaven and on earth has been given to me. Go therefore and make disciples of all nations, baptizing them in the name of the Father and of the Son and of the Holy Spirit, teaching them to observe all that I have commanded you. And behold, I am with you always, to the end of the age." (Matt. 28:18–20)

Jesus called his followers to go out and make disciples, teaching them to obey all that they had learned from him. Discipleship begins with evangelism, but it doesn't end there. As we study and learn truths about God, we continually pass on to others what we've received. Mentoring is a specific type of discipleship relationship. Through mentoring, an older believer teaches a younger believer how to walk by faith in obedience to God's commands.

Equipping for Ministry

Ephesians 4:11–13 explains the importance of growing in faith for the building up of the church:

> He gave the apostles, the prophets, the evangelists, the shepherds and teachers, *to equip the saints for the work of ministry, for building up the body of Christ,* until we all attain to the unity of the faith and of the knowledge of the Son of God, to mature manhood, to the measure of the stature of the fullness of Christ.

The apostle, prophet, evangelist, shepherd, and teacher have a shared goal in their training: to equip the saints for the work of ministry in hopes of building up the body of Christ. While this passage addresses those in official roles, we're all instructed to teach one another (Col. 3:16), and women are specifically called to teach other women (Titus 2:3–4).

There are two important aims we can glean from this passage as it applies to mentoring. A mentoring relationship seeks to:

- Equip a younger believer
- Encourage the work of ministry

Both of these concepts are vital for well-balanced discipleship. A woman needs to be equipped for ministry as well as actively participate in ministry in order to grow in maturity. A mentor is not just equipping for some imagined future service; she is equipping while she encourages a younger woman in her current ministry.

If either concept of discipleship is neglected, our mentoring can get off-kilter. If a woman is equipped but not participating in ministry, it is easy to become overconfident and self-focused. She quickly forgets why she even needs to be equipped because she doesn't truly understand how much she doesn't understand! If you can remember all the way back to high school algebra—often it's not until we take a test that we realize we've been overconfident in our understanding of the material.

Another problem arising from a woman being equipped without actively engaging in ministry is that she quickly loses interest in training. If a sports team only practiced but never participated in a real game, players would quickly get bored and lose interest in working diligently while in practice. The desire to train is actually increased by playing in the game and understanding areas of necessary growth. A key means of growth in the spiritual life involves actively participating in some form of ministry.

On the other side of the coin, if a woman only involves herself in ministry and never takes the time to be equipped, she may find herself struggling in different ways. She's equivalent to the sports team that never trains but only shows up for the game. She wears out quickly and has little stamina. She's unprepared for certain situations because she hasn't taken time outside of the game to consider the unexpected. In ministry the unequipped will quickly burn out and face exhaustion. Her external service lacks the internal strength and understanding needed to persevere well in her ministry to others.

Both sides of the definition—being equipped and actively participating in ministry—are vital for full-orbed discipleship. For women, Paul also gives a specific encouragement for mentoring, in his letter to Titus. He writes:

> Older women likewise are to be reverent in behavior, not slanderers or slaves to much wine. They are to teach what is good, and so train the young women to love their husbands and children, to be self-controlled, pure, working at home, kind, and submissive to their own husbands, that the word of God may not be reviled. (Titus 2:3–4)

Here we have a special exhortation for older women as they train the younger women. We'll refer to this passage more in the next chapter, but for clarity—this encouragement from Paul isn't a *limitation* on mentoring but a *special exhortation* for mentoring. Paul is not saying, "Only mentor women who are married and have young children." He also never says that mentors must be married and have children of their own. Jesus's final words in the Great Commission call us to make disciples, regardless of their gender, age, or marital status.

Paul is simply giving a special exhortation to older women as they mentor younger women who are married with children. It's tempting as a young wife and mom to believe that work in the home is insignificant in comparison to worldly accolades or more visible forms of ministry. Older women can encourage younger women by reminding them that the home is a vital place to bear fruit. Notice how many of the fruit of the Spirit are mentioned in the Titus 2 passage: goodness, love, self-control, and kindness. All believers should exhibit these fruit as they grow in faith. Paul is emphasizing—but not limiting—the importance of bearing these in the home.

For Unity and Maturity

Ephesians 4:11–13 also helps us understand that mentoring involves more than simply developing a friendship with an older or younger woman. It is designed to bring unity in the faith, knowledge of Christ, and maturity that overflows into a secure and stable trust in God that withstands the enemy's attacks. Unity is built as we grow together in truth and serve together in love. Maturity produces stability "so that we may no longer be children, tossed to and fro by the waves and carried about by every wind of doctrine, by human cunning, by craftiness in deceitful schemes" (Eph. 4:14).

Over time, the younger woman's faith strengthens so that she is no longer tossed back and forth by various teaching. She'll be able to discern what is best because she's been equipped. She'll have situational wisdom because she's participated in the work of ministry. Firmly rooted, she can stand beside others, helping them grow in godliness.

For God's Glory

As we mentor, it's important to keep our primary goal in mind. Ultimately, we want to help a younger woman grow in Christlikeness so that she glorifies God in all she does. We're not attempting to make others in our own image, crafting them to be like us. My goal isn't to make disciples of Melissa; I'm making disciples of Jesus.

John the Baptist understood his role and rejoiced when people left him to follow Jesus, saying, "He must increase, but I must decrease" (John 3:30). Our goal is to point people to Jesus, saying, "Go follow him. He's the source of all that is good!" As a younger woman beholds her King, she increasingly transforms into his likeness (2 Cor. 3:18).

Practically, this concept allows the mentor to work with diligence as well as rest with confidence. Her labors join with God's purpose for the women she mentors. By pointing another woman to Jesus, she knows her work is not in vain.

She rests with confidence because the work is ultimately God's, not her own. God forms and fashions his child in his timing. The mentor is freed from the pressure of perfection, because she is not the ultimate source of growth. She is supporting the work God is already doing. To refer back to our original metaphor, one tree cannot make another tree grow. It simply stands beside a younger tree and offers its strength for a season.

In Titus 2, Paul speaks to a variety of believers regarding their growth in righteousness. He explains the threefold purpose for equipping the saints for the work of ministry: God's word is upheld, the church is praised, and the gospel is adorned. The goal of mentoring is much larger than our personal happiness or growth. The goal is God's glory.

Ultimately this greater goal leads to our personal joy and growth, but it is a by-product of a much more important desire: God's name being declared holy in all the earth. This longing is the first request that Jesus teaches us to pray in the Lord's Prayer ("Hallowed be your name," Matt. 6:9), and it will be our greatest joy in all eternity. When God is rightly glorified, all will be well.

Biblical Examples of Mentoring

I always enjoy reading Christian biographies because they give me a greater vision of what it means to walk by faith. I've learned so much from their examples, and I've been inspired by their stories. Thankfully, the Bible offers us helpful examples of mentoring relationships that we can learn from: Mary and Elizabeth; Timothy and Paul; Peter, James, John, and Jesus.

My favorite example of a mentoring relationship is the one between Moses and Joshua. Joshua became Moses's aid during his youth (Num. 11:28). He served with Moses as a warrior, fighting the Amalekites while Moses raised his staff in prayer. He alone accompanied Moses onto Mount Sinai when Moses was given the

Ten Commandments (Ex. 24:12–15). When Moses would leave the tent of meeting, Joshua remained inside until he returned (Ex. 33:11). Moses included Joshua as one of the twelve men sent out to spy on the land of Canaan (Num. 13:16). Of the twelve, only Joshua and Caleb believed that the Lord could accomplish what he had promised. They were the only two men in their generation who were allowed to enter into the Promised Land (Num. 14:30, 38).

Toward the end of their ministry together, Moses repeatedly encouraged Joshua by reminding him that God would be faithful to fight the battles for the Israelites as they entered the Promised Land, just as he had done during their time wandering in the wilderness (Deut. 3:21–29). At the end of Moses's life, God commanded Moses to lay hands on Joshua and commission him before the entire assembly of the Israelites as God's chosen leader (Num. 27:18). Moses gave this final encouragement to Joshua:

> Be strong and courageous, for you shall go with this people into the land that the LORD has sworn to their fathers to give them, and you shall put them in possession of it. It is the LORD who goes before you. He will be with you; he will not leave you or forsake you. Do not fear or be dismayed. (Deut. 31:7–8)

The relationship between Moses and Joshua spanned decades and is one of the most vividly described mentoring relationships in all of Scripture. While most discipleship relationships will be much shorter in duration, we can glean several ideas that correspond with our earlier definition of mentoring from Ephesians.

Moses didn't spend forty years teaching Joshua truths about God and *then* send him out to lead the Israelites. His instruction and encouragement to Joshua came throughout years of active service on Joshua's part. As Joshua fought the Amalekites, sat in the tent of meeting, and spied out the land of Canaan, God prepared him as a leader. Joshua was learning from Moses as he was serving God.

Mentoring allows those already serving in the church to be built up so that they can be prepared for even greater service. If we think back to our tree analogy, the younger tree was already growing before it was tethered to the older tree. The stronger tree doesn't make the weaker tree grow, but it can help the younger tree grow upward in the right direction and provide protection from the elements surrounding it. Mentoring younger women who are already actively serving allows them preparation for the good works the Lord will call them to in future ministry.

A second principle we can observe between Moses and Joshua is that Moses brought Joshua with him as he engaged in ministry. Sometimes a younger woman can learn simply by serving alongside an older woman in what she is doing. It might be helpful to involve a younger woman while cooking a meal, setting up chairs, teaching a Sunday school class, helping on the finance committee, caring for an aging parent, or by attending a prayer meeting. Inviting a younger woman to come along as you serve others is an easy way to teach as you do ministry.

The final principle to consider is the way Moses regularly encouraged Joshua with his words. Moses was *for* Joshua. He wanted him to do well so that God's kingdom would advance. He knew that Joshua would face difficult adversaries, but he also knew God would be with Joshua. Moses reminded Joshua that God was for him and that God would accomplish all he called Joshua to do.

Through Moses's example, we find one of the most important roles of a mentor: she reminds the younger woman that God is with her and for her. While the storm winds may blow and the way seems unclear, God is leading and will direct her path. A mentor can shine the light of God's truth into the places where the younger woman may be tempted to doubt God's goodness.

Types of Mentoring

The relationship between Moses and Joshua is just one example of mentoring. No two mentoring relationships are the same, and there are a variety of ways to mentor. We benefit from both informal and more formal mentoring relationships. My relationship with Tracy happened naturally as I took part in FCA and became a student leader in the group. We never had a formal time together, but she mentored me as we shared life together.

When I was a freshman at the University of North Carolina, a woman named Deanne served as the staff worker from my chapter of InterVarsity Christian Fellowship. Early in the fall she approached me and asked me if I would like to meet once a week so that she could mentor me. Our relationship consisted of a regularly scheduled meeting, and we reevaluated at the end of each semester whether we both had the availability to continue meeting. Over the course of the next three years, we studied different books of the Bible together each week while sharing our lives and ministry in a personal way.

Both of these relationships proved extremely significant for me. My relationship with Deanne was not any less personal because it was more scheduled, nor was my relationship with Tracy any less impactful because it was more informal. An older woman can have a wonderful influence in mentoring a younger woman just by inviting her to go for a walk, being available to answer questions over coffee, or offering to hold a baby so she can have a hands-free moment. Over time, these older women mentor by their example of godliness and the biblical advice they pass on in conversations.

In this book, I hope to provide a path for women looking for a more structured approach to mentoring. It's a starting place both for women who want to mentor others and for women longing to be mentored. Essentially, what I hope to provide is the rope that will enable the older oak to be tethered to the younger tree. My intent isn't to offer the only way to mentor but to help provide a path for two women to walk together while focusing on knowing the Lord and growing in his likeness.

We've covered a lot on the topic of mentoring so far. We've explored the definition of mentoring, observed biblical examples and exhortations of mentoring, and considered the larger goals of mentoring. In the next chapter we'll begin to consider the practicalities of mentoring. Whom should I mentor? Whom should I seek out as a mentor? When should we meet and for how long? What should I expect our time together to look like? Setting reasonable expectations is vital for a positive mentoring experience.

Mentoring takes time, thoughtfulness, and effort. As you consider beginning this type of discipleship, let me encourage you that it's worth it. Paul emboldened the Corinthians in their labor by exhorting them, "Therefore, my beloved brothers, be steadfast, immovable, always abounding in the work of the Lord, knowing that in the Lord your labor is not in vain" (1 Cor. 15:58). As we mentor, we build up the church. Let us abound in this work, knowing that in the Lord our labors are never in vain.

2

Setting Expectations and Sharing Your Story

[The Lord] emboldens me to allow younger women to see not only my trials and sins but also how I respond as God brings me through them. It is through this kind of vulnerability that I learn to make my life an open book to the women I disciple. I learn to trust God's good purposes for my own struggles and receive his comfort for myself so I can in turn comfort others.

—*Kristie Anyabwile*

My hallway closet used to be a complete mess. Old towels, unmatched sheet sets, pillows, and a random assortment of gifts were all stuffed together, overflowing on every shelf. I hated opening the closet for fear of what might fall out.

Last summer I finally took everything out and divided the stuff into three piles: toss, donate, and keep. After taking out items to donate and throw away, I carefully placed everything else back in the closet. Now when I walk by the closet, I breathe a sigh of relief. I love opening it up and seeing everything in its place.

This chapter is somewhat like cleaning that closet. It may not be exactly thrilling to discuss organizational details, but doing so on the front end of a mentoring relationship can help prevent unrealized expectations from spilling out months later. The work you put into this chapter will help organize your time together in a way that yields unity and understanding rather than division and disappointment.

We'll consider three important topics: setting expectations, considering gospel-centered discipleship, and taking the plunge to share your stories with each other. Honesty in each of these areas opens the door for a healthy relationship.

Setting Expectations

Communication is important in any relationship but especially in a mentoring relationship. After months of meeting with one woman, I realized we had completely different expectations of what mentoring should look like. In her mind, I wasn't living up to what she had hoped for in a mentor. In my mind, she wasn't putting the time and effort into our meetings. She was hoping to spend time together and hang out as friends. I was asking her to work through a Bible study curriculum and found myself frustrated that she never completed the homework. We didn't have a regularly scheduled meeting time, and eventually our relationship fizzled into an awkward, "Hey, we should catch up sometime!"

I learned a lot from my failure in that relationship. When she asked to meet, I had a vision of what our time together would look like. So did she. However, we never communicated about the goal of our time together. She wanted a relationship with me, and I wanted to help grow her relationship with God. We started off with different goals and no clear path forward.

Since then, I've changed the way I mentor in two important ways. The first is to set an expected frequency and duration for time together. I encourage you to set a specific date, time, and location. Will you meet once a month, twice a month, or once a week? Perhaps you'll meet the first Tuesday of every month for breakfast or every other Thursday evening for dessert. Figure out what day and time works best for you both and then commit to that time together.

I also encourage you to consider a specific duration for how long you'll meet, and later you can reevaluate if need be. It may be six months, it may be a year, or it may be until you finish this book, but it's good to have a set time based on both of your schedules.

One fear of mentoring (for both people) is that it's a lifelong commitment! Just like two trees aren't tethered together forever, mentoring relationships are often seasonal. This reality doesn't mean the relationship ends. Last summer my high school FCA leader Tracy and I spent a weekend with our families at the lake. It's been over twenty-five years since we lived in the same city, but we could pick right back up talking about family, faith, and ministry. Just because you may not meet every week for the rest of your lives doesn't mean that the relationship is less than it used to be. It just takes on different contours in different seasons.

Since we're setting expectations, it's also good to clearly define what each person expects of the other in the relationship. Basically, we want to consider: How can the mentor be faithful in her mentoring, and how can the mentee be faithful in her learning?

A Word to the Mentor

Your Example Matters

In his letter to Titus, Paul writes, "Older women likewise are to be reverent in behavior, not slanderers or slaves to much wine. They are to teach what is good" (Titus 2:3). Paul isn't demanding perfection (none of us would pass that test!), but he does want the older women to be faithful examples as they teach younger women. Some questions to consider as you think about this passage from Titus:

- *Reverent in the way she lives*: Do I give thought to my ways? Do I use my time to serve others? Does my life increasingly reflect my faith? (How do I live?)

- *Not slanderers*: Do I display wisdom with my words? Do I gossip? Do I speak well of others close to me? Do I complain frequently? (How do I speak?)

- *Not slaves*: Do I possess inner discipline regarding alcohol, food, exercise, TV, shopping, and other worldly pleasures? Do I increasingly trust in God for my joy and contentment? (What governs my affections?)

- *Teaches what is good*: Do I give worldly advice or biblical wisdom? Do I have a regular practice of Bible reading and prayer? Do I faithfully seek ways to grow in my own knowledge and understanding? (What governs my mind?)

You may read that list and want to quietly turn and run as fast as you can away from being a mentor. Please don't! Perfection is impossible. However, we can be women who seek to love God in all we think, say, and do. That's what your mentee needs most: a woman who earnestly desires to know God and glorify him with her life.

Involve and Invite

One of the best ways you can share your life with the woman you're discipling is to invite her into and involve her in your life. One little poem that someone passed on to me goes something like this:

I do, you watch.
I do, you help.
You do, I help.
You do, I watch.

As you minister in your local church, bring your mentee along. If you're teaching a Bible study or Sunday school class, involve her in some way. If you're serving in a soup kitchen or visiting at the jail, ask her if she can join you. If you're running errands on a Saturday, see if she wants to ride along with you. If you're watching your kids play sports, ask her to come and chat with you on the sidelines. If you're heading out for a walk, see if she can join you. Inviting her into your real life—even the piles of laundry and many messy moments—will help her feel comfortable sharing her life with you.

Follow Up

If the woman you're mentoring asks you to hold her accountable or shares a difficult part of her story, make sure to follow up with her in the next few days. Sharing parts of our past can make us feel unlovable or unworthy. You may be the first person she opens up to about past sin, past hurts, or broken dreams. Meet her with love, acceptance, and grace as she shares. And if she needs accountability for current sin struggles, give her that. Knowing that you'll ask about these struggles may be just what she needs to help her in the fight.

Pray Regularly

Our prayers for one another are a gift. Pray regularly for the woman you're discipling. If you come across a verse in your own study that is applicable to your discussions, send it to her and pray it for her. When you are struggling to know how to help, ask God to give you wisdom and discernment. Cling to his promise, "If any of you lacks wisdom, let him ask God, who gives generously to all without reproach, and it will be given him" (James 1:5).

Be encouraged—the work you do by investing in another woman matters. You may not always see fruit immediately, but the Lord is at work in you and through you as you offer support to a younger woman.

A Word to the Mentee

Be Faithful

Whatever you've decided to study or read, be faithful to complete the assignments. Your mentor is offering you her time, energy, and care. You'll only grow as much as you put into the relationship. Don't skip the time with her because something more fun appears on your social calendar. Spiritual growth doesn't just happen. As one of my mentors used to say, "You don't drift toward holiness." Choose to be faithful in this relationship, knowing it is a blessing in your life. Be on time, show up, and be thankful.

Be Active, Not Passive

Be active, not passive in the mentoring process. Don't assume your mentor will always know exactly what you need. Think through what you'd like to ask her and bring questions to your time together. When you're having a hard day, let her know and ask her to pray for you. When you're faced with a difficult decision, ask her advice. Invite her into your life and listen to the wisdom she has to offer.

Be Honest and Humble

You don't have to hide your struggles from your mentor. Be honest. Confess when you've sinned and ask for help. When your mentor provides accountability and offers insight into sin patterns, listen with humility. It may be difficult to hear, but be willing to receive her advice and correction. Proverbs reminds us: "Faithful are the wounds of a friend" (Prov. 27:6). Her accountability is a kindness (even though it may be painful at times) and will help you grow together in godliness.

Be Caring and Understanding

It's important to find ways to care for and encourage the woman mentoring you. She has struggles of her own that she is facing. Even though her life may look orderly and together, she probably feels overwhelmed many days. When you call to ask for help, make sure to ask her how she's doing. When she's having a difficult day, stop by with her favorite coffee or some flowers. Write her a note, letting her know how her words of advice have helped you. Be considerate and caring toward her, knowing she has her own defeats, struggles, insecurities, and hardships.

Be Prayerful

Your mentor needs your prayers just as you need hers. Each time you meet, ask her how you can pray for her. My intern asks me to share my rose, bud, and thorn from the past week or two. My rose is something good that's happened, my bud is something that I'm looking forward to, and my thorn is something difficult I'm facing. This simple activity has allowed me to share parts of my life with her that I might not have taken the time to do if she hadn't asked. I've felt so cared for in our times together to know she's praying for me in these areas.

As you meet with your mentor, I encourage you to continue to grow in every other way you can. You'll be amazed at how the Lord will meet you as you hear the word preached, share in Communion, listen in Sunday school, spend time studying the Bible, and serve faithfully in your church. God will providentially arrange these various areas in surprising ways that will collectively help to grow your faith.

Gospel-Centered Discipleship

At the end of this chapter, I've provided a list of questions to help you both share your stories with each other. Some of you may be unsure about where you are in your faith. You may be exploring

Christianity for the first time, or you may have grown up in the church but find yourself wondering if it's true. It's okay to share your doubts, questions, and concerns. You don't have to have it all figured out. Keep praying that God will reveal himself to you.

Others may be afraid to share because of fear or guilt. You may have things like abuse, addiction, abortion, greed, lying, or cheating in your story. Shame causes us to hide. Remember this truth from Paul: "And such were some of you. But you were washed, you were sanctified, you were justified in the name of the Lord Jesus Christ and by the Spirit of our God" (1 Cor. 6:11). Christ is redeeming your story. You're not enslaved to it any longer.

We're all equal at the foot of the cross. All have sinned and fallen short of the glory of God. We all need Jesus to rescue us. For all who have believed by faith, we can rejoice in these words: "There is therefore now no condemnation for those who are in Christ Jesus. For the law of the Spirit of life has set you free in Christ Jesus from the law of sin and death" (Rom. 8:1–2). No matter what you've done, Jesus's blood is sufficient.

Sin no longer condemns, and it's no longer your master. The Spirit awakens new life with new desires. Yes, we still struggle with sin. The battle isn't yet finished. Currently the penalty of sin and the power of sin are defeated in the life of a Christian. However, not until heaven will we be removed from sin's presence. We're still at war: our flesh battles with our spirit to walk in obedience to Jesus. This reality is true for both older Christians and younger Christians. We're in the fight together.

As you open your lives up to each other, live in the freedom of the gospel. You're not defined by your past actions but by Christ's redemptive work in your life. Share freely how he's been at work. It takes courage, but it's worth it.

Sharing Your Story

Below you'll find ten questions for you both to answer and then discuss when you meet. It's helpful to write down your answers beforehand so that you'll have already considered what's most important to share. I know we can't share all of our stories (that might take a while!), but I'm always amazed at how doing this simple activity together leads to an open and honest mentoring relationship. It's a great way to get to know each other and helps give insight into all the other topics we'll discuss in the upcoming chapters.

"Sharing Your Story" Questions

1. How did you become a Christian? If you're not sure if you're a Christian, what keeps you from believing in Jesus?

2. What ministry, person, or book has God used to deepen your faith?

3. Is there a particular verse, passage, or book of Scripture that you would consider significant in your life? Why?

4. What ways do you enjoy serving in ministry? What would you consider your spiritual gifts? How have you seen God prepare you for the ministry he has called you to do?

5. What was your family like? How does your relationship with your family members impact or influence your relationship with God and others?

6. If you're single, do you live alone or have a roommate? Who are the people you primarily live life with? What are some of the struggles of singleness you've experienced, and what are some of the joys? If you're married, how did you meet your husband? How would you describe your marriage? What struggles have you gone through or do you currently face?

7. What sin patterns do you struggle to overcome? Do you have unconfessed sin in your life that you need to address?

8. What truth about God supports you in times of struggle or trial? What trials have affected your life and how have you received comfort from the Lord in them?

9. How has knowing Jesus made a difference in your life? How would you describe your affection for him at this point in your life—vibrant, warm, lukewarm, cold, indifferent, angry, or fearful?

10. How would you like to grow in your faith in the coming year? What particular area would you like to see progress?

Take a few moments to pray for one another, thanking God for the ways he has worked in the past to give you faith and bring you to himself. Ask him for continued growth in wisdom, knowledge, and faith as you meet together over the next nine chapters. May the Lord bless, encourage, and strengthen you both as you grow together in Christ.

3

Taste and See

Savoring the Word of God

God never requires submission to a harmful command. None of his commands are harmful. In commanding what brings him glory he commands what ultimately brings us good. He can only use his authority for good.

—Jen Wilkin

Typically I'm not one for reading instructions, particularly when it comes to electronics. Most devices are made in such a way that how they work seems pretty obvious, right? However, sometimes my failure to read instructions leads to mounting frustration and wasted time. While heading out of town a few weeks ago, both my daughter and I were out of data on our phones (a typical struggle for the two of us). We decided to connect my husband's phone to the Bluetooth in the car so we could play the music we wanted— John Denver's "Country Roads" (to be specific).

I did everything I knew to do to connect that phone. We pressed numerous buttons, turned the phone on and off, disconnected and reconnected his Bluetooth, disconnected all other phones from the device list on the car. Nothing worked. Eventually I pulled out the instruction manual for the car and started reading. After about one minute I read, "New devices can only be paired when the car is in Park."

Big sigh.

All my attempts at figuring out what was wrong were in vain because I didn't understand how the car worked. Even though I considered myself fairly tech savvy, my understanding was insufficient. I needed the wisdom of the person who created the car to really know how the car worked and understand why it wasn't doing what I wanted it to do.

It's like that with our lives in general, isn't it? We usually think we know how we work best, but then we find ourselves frustrated that our lives aren't working properly. There's a good reason. We actually don't know how we work best. As much as we'd like to think we know ourselves, our understanding is limited. We're created beings, which means we have a creator.

God knows exactly what we need, and he's revealed truth to us through his word. God's word is described as a light to our path, a lamp for our feet—it illuminates our way like nothing else can (Ps. 119:105). For that reason, we'll spend this chapter considering why God's word is so important for our spiritual growth, the ways unbelief keeps us from our Bible, and the good news for grace-filled living.

Wisdom for Life

There are so many options available for us to learn God's word. At church we hear the word preached. At home we can read it for ourselves. Most churches have small groups where the Bible is studied with others. We can memorize and meditate on passages so that we marinate in the text and really get to know what the Bible says.

We have so many resources and study methods available to us, but we often fail to take advantage of them because at some level we really don't think reading, studying, memorizing, meditating on, and learning God's word is all that important. Our lives are busy, we're tired, and sometimes we wonder if an ancient book has modern-day relevance.

For that reason, let's begin by considering the Bible's importance, necessity, and relevance. God's word is able to do all these things—and so much more.

Make You Wise for Salvation

You may be in a mentoring relationship, but you might not be sure what you believe about Christianity. Or perhaps you consider yourself a Christian but wonder fearfully at times, *Am I really a believer? Do I have saving faith?* When Paul wrote to Timothy about his faith, he mentioned that Timothy had known the Scriptures from childhood and that they were "able to make [him] wise for salvation through faith in Christ Jesus" (2 Tim. 3:15).

If you don't know exactly what you believe, the best way to begin is reading the Bible for yourself. There are numerous plans to help you read through the Bible in a year, or you could start by studying one book of the Bible. There are many excellent study guides that can help lead you through a book. Ask your mentor for her favorite suggestions! I regularly use study guides and have found they help me go deeper into God's word just through the questions they pose about the text. In the appendix of this book, I've provided a list of resources to help you dig in to the Bible on your own.

Grow Your Relationship with God

All relationships take time to build. Friends plan times to get together and catch up. Spouses reconnect on date nights. Church members chat over potluck dinners. Building fellowship with others takes time. If we want to grow a friendship with God, we need time in his presence for that relationship to flourish. Reading the Bible on a daily basis allows us the opportunity to get to know God: What does he care about? How does he respond? Whom does he love?

The Bible alone offers answers to these questions, because the Bible reveals the character of God. Don't think of God as a friend of a friend. You can get to know him for yourself by reading, studying, and meditating on his word. What a gift for us to be able to get to know him! You may be surprised at how much more wonderful (and complex) he is than you originally thought.

Help You Fight Temptation

We all struggle with sin. The Bible offers stories of imperfect people: liars, adulterers, murderers, and idolaters. We're told that these stories were written for our benefit: "Now these things took place as examples for us, that we might not desire evil as they did" (1 Cor. 10:1–13).

The Bible illuminates our propensity toward sin as well as prepares us to fight it. The word of God acts as a sword against the attacks of the devil (Eph. 6:17). The psalmist tells us, "I have stored up your word in my heart, that I might not sin against you" (Ps. 119:11). Being in the word on a daily basis strengthens our minds, fortifying and preparing our hearts for the battle that will surely come our way. In addition to reading and studying, memorizing Bible passages can help prepare our minds for action.

Provide Revival, Wisdom, and Joy

Are you weary? Unsure of what to do? In need of wisdom in some area? Just take a moment to read the promises found in Psalm 19:7–11:

The law of the LORD is perfect, reviving the soul;
   the testimony of the LORD is sure, making wise the
      simple;
the precepts of the LORD are right, rejoicing the heart;
   the commandment of the LORD is pure, enlightening
      the eyes.

We miss out on so much when we neglect the Bible. Soul refreshment doesn't come from a Netflix binge, a fancy vacation, or hours on social media. Wisdom doesn't come from reading all the self-help books in the library. Joy doesn't come from getting the Next Best Thing. Enlightenment doesn't come from traveling the world and having new experiences.

What a gift God has given us in his word! Revival, wisdom, joy, and enlightenment—these are the treasures we uncover as we mine the riches of God's word. God is the source of all we need, and he's given us his word so that we can experience abundant life and unfailing joy.

Nourish Your Soul

Psalm 1 tells us that the man who delights in the law of the Lord is like a "tree planted by streams of water, that yields its fruit in season, and its leaf does not wither. In all that he does, he prospers." Isaiah 55 compares time with the Lord to a feast in which we delight our souls in the richest of fare. Jesus told us that abiding in him was more necessary than food or water because apart from him, we can do nothing (John 15:1–5). However, in Christ we can do all things (Phil. 4:13).

There's a lot of talk in the world today about self-care. There are numerous articles and books about eating right, sleeping right, and taking the time to exercise. While these are all important parts of maintaining a healthy physical body, our souls need care. God's word is nourishment and sustenance for your soul like healthy food is for your body. In a world that encourages you to "treat yourself," the most important gift you can give yourself is time with Jesus in his word.

Provide Comfort

Each of us will suffer. Many false assurances of happiness and ease are the result of misapplied promises born out of an insufficient understanding of God's word. Knowing God's promises, in the full context of his word, helps us to put our hope in God and find comfort for our souls in times of hardship and distress. The psalmist tells us, "This is my comfort in my affliction, that your promise gives me life" (Ps. 119:50). When the storm winds blow the strongest, we'll be thankful for an anchor buried deep within the promises of God.

Transform You to Look Like Christ

When I was in college, I lived with the same roommate for four years. Eventually we began to look alike, talk alike, and use similar mannerisms. Time together made us become like each other. In a similar way, time with Jesus makes us look like Jesus. The Bible is not simply a textbook to teach us facts about Jesus. It's living and active. We actually meet with Jesus as we spend time in his word.

We live in the age of information. However, the most brilliant insights of men or women are from the minds of created beings. In the Bible, we have access to the wisdom of an infinite God and Creator, the one who knows all things and understands the beginning from the end. What a privilege to come and learn from him. Don't miss it! As our minds are renewed, our lives are transformed (Rom. 12:2).

Bless You to Be a Blessing

As the Bible transforms us, we become living examples of Jesus to the world around us. We share our faith, care for the poor, work with diligence, extend mercy, love unconditionally, forgive those who sin against us, confess our sins, and shine as lights in a dark and weary world. If we want to impact the world, we must first be impacted by the word.

If you are thirsty for more, you're invited to a feast. For all of these benefits, and many more, God invites you:

> Come, everyone who thirsts,
>> come to the waters;
> and he who has no money,
>> come, buy and eat!
> Come, buy wine and milk
>> without money and without price.
> Why do you spend your money for that which is not bread,
>> and your labor for that which does not satisfy?
> Listen diligently to me, and eat what is good,
>> and delight yourselves in rich food.
> Incline your ear, and come to me;
>> hear, that your soul may live. (Isa. 55:1–3)

Wandering in Unbelief

With all these benefits, you'd think Bible reading would be a top priority. However, a 2017 Barna study reported that while 87 percent of American homes have a Bible, only 20 percent of people are Bible engaged, meaning they read, use, or listen to the Bible four times a week or more.[3] Here's the truth of our situation: we have access to God's word, but it's not regularly read in our homes.

Why do we neglect God's word? For each person, the reasons may be different, but I think there are some common objections— whispers of unbelief—that we tell ourselves, rather than listen to the wisdom of God.

Objection 1: "I Don't Have Time"

I know. I know. It's so difficult to think about adding anything into your already crammed full, struggling-to-survive kind of days. I feel it too. Life takes a lot of time. There's work to be done, friends to see, books to read, service to be offered, and pleasures to be enjoyed. We may feel overwhelmed, but we have to be brave enough to speak this truth to ourselves:

I do not have a busyness problem. I have a belief problem.

We spend our lives on what we really believe will bring satisfaction. If it's our families, then we'll make our homes the center of our world. If it's our work, we'll scramble and work until all hours of the night to get it done. If it's our comforts, we'll seek food, vacations, entertainment, and pleasures to try to fill ourselves. We are thirsty creatures seeking satisfaction. We'll take a drink from whatever fount we most believe offers us relief.

You need Jesus. Fight for time with him. Believe that he is the one thing needed and trust him for everything else. And know this—he will not make you lack in the other areas in which you long. He will fill them in such a beautiful way that you will be more joyful in your relationships, work, and comforts because you have first found your satisfaction in him.

Objection 2: "I Always End Up Quitting, and I Feel Like a Failure"

Don't let your past bind you with fear. Perfection isn't the goal. Instead, try to develop healthy patterns of Bible reading. Perhaps this year you'll make it a little further than last year. And maybe next year you'll finish that study guide or Bible reading plan. Don't quit before you've already begun because you're concerned about failure. You can become a woman who reads the Bible regularly, and it's worth every attempt.

If you've struggled with daily Bible reading in the past, I encourage you to grab a few friends and try to read through the Bible together. Our assistant pastor did this with a group of us a few years ago. We formed a private Facebook group, and once every few months he would check in to see how it was going, and we would share with one another what we were learning. Just like exercise is easier when you do it with a friend, faithful Bible reading flourishes in loving community. Don't let fear of failure keep you from enjoying God in new ways.

Objection 3: "I Get Bored and Confused"

Yes, most likely you will find yourself bored or confused somewhere along the way. I always do. Keep reading. Sometimes the slowness of the narrative suddenly awakens you to the gospel in a new way. Or you may spend days in confusion and then a small connection with another part brings clarity. *Let the confusion awaken your curiosity.*

True learning takes place when all seems dark. That's why teachers always talk about seeing "the light go on" in someone's eyes. Being in the dark is just the moment before understanding happens. Keep reading. The Spirit is your tutor, and the word is alive. God will meet you.

Objection 4: "I Already Know a Lot about God and the Bible"

This objection may not be one that most of us would speak out loud. However, somewhere within our hearts we hear the false whisper, *You already know God; why do you need to know more about him?*

Our feelings of adequacy in our understanding are probably the most convincing evidence of how little we know about God. Paul (who clearly knew God) told the Philippians, "I want to know Christ" (Phil. 3:10 NIV). The most mature saints are often the ones who realize how little they know of God. The more they read, the more they exclaim, "Oh the depth of the riches and wisdom and knowledge of God! How unsearchable are his judgments and how inscrutable his ways!" (Rom. 11:33).

They've tasted God's goodness, and they want more.

God is the subject of all eternity, and we can spend a lifetime seeking to know him more. As Puritan author John Flavel explained:

It is profound; all other sciences are but shadows; this is a boundless, bottomless ocean; no creature has a line long enough to fathom its depths; there is height, length, depth, and breadth ascribed to it, yea it passes knowledge. Eternity itself cannot fully unfold him. It is like exploring a newly discovered land; by degrees you search further and further into the heart of the country. Ah, the best of us are yet on the borders of this vast continent! The study of Jesus Christ is the noblest subject that ever a soul spent itself upon.[4]

There is no better pursuit than knowing God. Don't stop before you even start. Plan to make this year a year of knowing him in new ways through his word.

Walking by Faith: Good News for Grace-Filled Living

Years ago I was traveling by myself on a three-hour car ride back to Charlotte after visiting my parents. The highway route was familiar, so I put the car on cruise control and began listening to music. At some point along the way, I began to notice something strange. The truck beside me seemed to be following me. Whenever I sped up or slowed down, he did the same. Whenever I switched lanes, he'd follow suit. It began to concern me, and I wondered to myself, *Why is he following me?*

The longer I drove, the more uncomfortable I became. The tension built in my shoulders as it began to rain, and the dusk settled in to darkness. As I strained to see the road ahead of me, my hands firmly gripped the steering wheel at ten and two. Rather than feel relaxed on my drive, I was constantly aware of his presence.

At some point, I suddenly realized why my eyes felt so strained—my car lights weren't on! I'd been driving in the darkness and rain without them. Quickly I turned on my lights, and as soon as I did, guess what happened? The truck immediately drove on his way. At that moment, I realized my mistake. I thought he'd been there with some malicious intent, following me. However, he'd actually been there to protect me, following along because he was concerned about me and wanted to make sure I was safe.

God's word is a lot like that truck. Many times, we're fearful of God's word and feel like it's pursuing us, telling us all the ways we fail to measure up. While the Bible does show us our sin, it's not to make us feel hopeless—it's to lead us to the good news of the gospel! The Bible illuminates our need for Jesus so that we'll seek him as our Savior.

Once the Holy Spirit opens our eyes through faith and turns on the lights, we have a new relationship with God's word. It may convict us, but it no longer condemns. God's word becomes a path for us to follow as we live life by the Spirit. We can come to the Bible with delight rather than fear because we know that the word is there to protect us, not to harm us.

Our faithfulness in Bible reading doesn't earn God's favor. In case you were wondering, there's no angel in heaven with a star chart keeping record of who read her Bible today. God doesn't love you more because you've read the Bible all the way through— God accepts you fully on the merits of Christ's perfect obedience. If you are in Christ, you are clothed in his righteousness. You are made perfect by his blood, not by your Bible reading.

But how am I assured of this truth? *I read it in the Bible.*

We don't spend time with God so that he will love us more. We spend time in the word because we need daily reminders of his love. We don't spend time with God so that he will show us favor. We spend time in the word because we need reminders of his favor freely given.

We are forgetful creatures, trying to survive on the crumbs of the world, when he's offered us a feast. I don't want you to read the Bible so you'll believe you've lived up to some sort of righteous standard. I hope you'll read the Bible so you'll feast on the joy of knowing God.

However, like all relationships it takes effort. It's normal that some days you won't feel like reading your Bible. That's okay—you can still read it. It's not legalistic to read your Bible even when you don't feel like it. Planning to meet with God each day is similar to planning a regular lunch date with a friend. We make the effort when we want to build the relationship. Choosing to meet with Jesus daily is a faithful act of belief. We cease from our own efforts and say to ourselves, *What I need more than anything else is time listening to God speak to me through his word.*

We begin by listening to his word, and then we obey it. On the night before he died, Jesus taught his disciples, "Abide in my love. If you keep my commandments, you will abide in my love, just as I have kept my Father's commandments and abide in his love. These things I have spoken to you, that my joy may be in you, and that your joy may be full" (John 15:9–11).

Take a moment to notice the relationship between love, obedience, and joy. Jesus isn't trying to make your life miserable by calling you to obey his word. He wants you to abide in his love and have fullness of joy! God doesn't give us his word to keep us from life. He gives us his word so we can walk in abundance of life.

We may think we know how we work best, but we don't. Jesus gives us his word and shows us how to live. The Spirit guides us in all these things so that we can be both hearers and doers of the word. May we walk by faith as we listen to the word, obey the word, and delight in the word.

Before You Meet: Practical Tools to Help You Grow

The Navigators is a ministry that has some excellent resources. I'm a visual learner, so one illustration that's been helpful for me is The Word Hand. Look up this diagram online (the link is provided in the notes).[5] Which of those ways of taking in God's word would you like to work on during the next month?

If you're looking for a way to help memorize Scripture on your phone, Bible Memory is an app that you might want to get.[6]

If you prefer to memorize with notecards, Verse Card Maker is an online tool that helps format notecards so you can print them out easily.[7]

If you'd like to read the Bible in a year, I highly recommend a five-day Bible reading plan that I describe in detail at The Gospel Coalition website.[8]

Another site that has some excellent resources to help you study the Bible on your own is Risen Motherhood (it's not only for moms!). The site offers worksheets to guide you as you read.[9]

Take about ten minutes and look up some of those websites before you meet. If you're looking for a Bible study, I've listed some options in the appendix for you to consider. There are great studies out there that can help teach you how to study the Bible as you study the Bible.

While You Meet: Questions for Discussion

1. On a scale of 1–10, with 1 being very uncomfortable and 10 being very comfortable, how comfortable do you feel reading the Bible on your own?

2. How do you study the Bible? Do you read it through in a year, use a study guide, or go through it on your own? Are there any study guides you've used in the past that have helped you study God's word?

3. Of the eight benefits given for Bible reading, which one have you experienced most? Is there a benefit that you struggle to see in your life?

4. How has God's word been a comfort to you in difficult times, or how has it helped you fight temptation? Is there a particular verse you turn to in trials? Temptations?

5. Which of the objections listed in the chapter keep you from reading your Bible on a regular basis?

6. In the upcoming year, how would you like to grow in knowing the Bible? Also discuss how to hold each other accountable in the upcoming year for how you'd like to grow. Would you like to:

   • Memorize a certain number of verses?
   • Read the Bible every day?
   • Study one book of the Bible more in-depth?
   • Obey God's word in a certain way?

Until You Meet Again: Growing in Godliness

Based on your discussion, consider one area in which you'd like to make a change before you meet next time. It could be to start doing something that will help you grow spiritually or to stop doing something that is preventing your growth. Write it in the space below and discuss it the next time you meet.

4

The Church

Our Home Away from Home

The church is not a human invention. . . . The church is established by Christ, protected and nourished by Christ, governed by Christ, and exists for the glory of Christ. Because of this, the church is also not optional. . . . The church is fundamental to the identity of everyone who belongs to Christ.

—*Megan Hill*

Years ago, when my husband was completing his PhD at the University of Edinburgh, my parents took us on a European bus tour as a surprise Christmas gift. It was the absolute best gift to give two people living overseas with plenty of time but little money. We traveled and visited sites all throughout England, France, Italy, Austria, Switzerland, and the Netherlands. In every city we visited, there was always a church or a cathedral on our tour. They were typically large and ornate, with beautiful stained-glass windows, each depicting some biblical story.

By the time we were about six days into the ten-day trip, we lost interest in the cathedrals. It was a bit of an "If you've seen one, you've seen them all" mentality. When I think of all the years it took to construct each of those buildings and the beautiful handiwork in every detail, it's somewhat embarrassing that we could so quickly lose interest. But after seeing so many, we took for granted the grandeur and wanted to move on to other things.

When we think about church in the life of a Christian, it's fairly easy to do the same thing I did on our European whirl. We quickly grow bored and dissatisfied or just take it for granted altogether. I'm not talking about the building we go to but about the people inside. Even though we typically think of a church as a structure or a meeting place, the real church is what the Bible refers to as the people of God. Churches (the buildings) got their name because that's the place the church (the people of God) met to worship God.

You may have a complicated relationship with the church. It's easy to grow discontent with God's people and think, *If you've seen one, you've seen them all*. Perhaps you're *church wounded*—people have hurt you or let you down and your trust of the church is at an all-time low. Perhaps you're *church fatigued*—weary and worn down from the grind of coming and going, and participating doesn't really seem to affect your life all that much. Maybe you're wondering if you need the church or if it needs you. Or perhaps you're *church dissatisfied* and looking over the fence and wondering if there's something better going on at the church down the street. Hopefully, some of you are *church healthy*—thankful to be a part of a gospel-centered body of believers who love one another and serve one another well. And maybe you're a mix of some combination of all of the above.

Whatever your current relationship with the church, we'll spend this chapter looking at why the church is so important in the life of a believer. With new technologies such as podcasts and livestreaming, you may be wondering if you need to be part of a church at all. It's easy to question, *Can't I just tune in when it's convenient?* In this chapter we want to consider the biblical purpose of the church, the reasons we wander from the church, and what it looks like to graciously build our lives as members of God's people.

Wisdom for Life

While the Gospels share the historical account of Jesus's life on earth, the book of Acts tells the history of the early church. Jesus ascended to heaven, and then the Spirit descended at Pentecost, anointing the disciples with tongues of fire and a divine call to build the church and fulfill the Great Commission. But they didn't get out hammers and nails and start a building project. Instead, they started preaching the good news of the gospel. As the word of God went out through their message, people came to faith.

Acts 2:41–46 describes what happened:

> So those who received his word were baptized, and there were added that day about three thousand souls. And they devoted themselves to the apostles' teaching and the fellowship, to the breaking of bread and the prayers. And awe came upon every soul, and many wonders and signs were being done through the apostles. And all who believed were together and had all things in common. And they were selling their possessions and belongings and distributing the proceeds to all, as any had need. And day by day, attending the temple together and breaking bread in their homes, they received their food with glad and generous hearts, praising God and having favor with all the people. And the Lord added to their number day by day those who were being saved.

That first day of preaching, three thousand believed the message and were baptized! They began to meet together and devoted themselves to God's word and to one another, shared Communion, prayed for each other, and cared for one another as they had need, all the while praising God. This description is a picture of the church.

What's amazing to me is that after two thousand years—while the church may have grown and spread to various cultures and continents—the basic building blocks of the church remain. The church is our home as believers. It's not enough for us to be a part of the invisible church (which consists of true believers all over the world); we need to commit ourselves to a local Bible-believing church. It's where we're baptized, celebrate Communion, hear God's word, build fellowship, pray, and worship God. Some churches are large, some have just a few families, but all share a common message (the gospel), common language (prayer), and common covenantal signs (Communion and baptism).

While the church may feel somewhat ordinary (just like I felt about cathedrals on my European trip), it's important that we don't take it for granted. God's handiwork is seen in every person he saves. He is designing and crafting something much more majestic than a physical building. He is shaping lives that together form a beautiful reflection of his Son. We are part of something greater than ourselves. We radiate together in a way that we could never do without one another. If you found one piece of stained glass, you might look at it for a moment as a trinket, but when it is set inside with other pieces, it illuminates a glorious story. You are incomplete without the church, and the church is incomplete without you.

The Bible explains the reasons each of us needs the church— we need the church's teaching, accountability, fellowship, and ministry.

Teaching and Instruction

In most of the Western world, we're blessed to have the Bible in our own language. We're not dependent upon someone reading God's word to us to enable us to know it for ourselves. However, we still need to hear the word taught and preached, and we need shepherds to guide us in the truth. As Paul wrote to the Ephesian church:

> He gave the apostles, the prophets, the evangelists, the shepherds and teachers, to equip the saints for the work of ministry, *for building up the body of Christ*, until we all attain to the unity of the faith and of the knowledge of the Son of God, to mature manhood, to the measure of the stature of the fullness of Christ, so that we may no longer be children, tossed to and fro by the waves and carried about by every wind of doctrine, by human cunning, by craftiness in deceitful schemes. Rather, speaking the truth in love, *we are to grow up in every way into him* who is the head, into Christ, from whom the whole body, joined and held together by every joint with which it is equipped, *when each part is working properly, makes the body grow so that it builds itself up in love*. (Eph. 4:11–16)

There's a lot in this passage, some of which we discussed in chapter 1. God gives the church shepherds and teachers to equip us for ministry so that we can build up one another in unity of faith and knowledge. We need biblical teaching so that we can serve and encourage others. We're linked together—how I'm doing affects how you're doing. It's impossible to be connected to Christ and not be connected to all the other parts of his body.

It's in the church that we'll find these teachers and shepherds. They teach us by both their words and their example. Hebrews 13:7 instructs us, "Remember your leaders, those who spoke to you the word of God. Consider the outcome of their way of life, and imitate their faith." In our day and age, we can listen to and learn from teachers all over the world. However, it's one thing to hear instruction taught. It's another to see love, joy, peace, patience, kindness, goodness, faithfulness, gentleness, and self-control in action. Observing these embodied qualities allows us opportunity to imitate the faith of our pastors. It's not enough to hear a sermon online or catch a podcast here or there. As we know the leaders in our church, we learn from both their instruction and their lives.

Accountability and Authority

Neither accountability nor authority is a popular word right now. Memes proclaim, "Reject authority," and, "Rules are made to be broken." Most children are quite comfortable telling others, "You're not the boss of me." However, just like children need parents, the church needs leaders and shepherds. Authority is given not to fuel the pride of the leader but to protect those they lead. Paul instructed leaders, "Pay careful attention to yourselves and to all the flock, in which the Holy Spirit has made you overseers to care for the church of God, which he obtained with his own blood. I know that after my departure fierce wolves will come in among you, not sparing the flock; and from among your own selves will arise men speaking twisted things, to draw away the disciples after them" (Acts 20:28–30).

Leaders are provided to care for the church. But it's also important to notice that false teachers (Paul calls them fierce wolves) will be among us, speaking twisted things. How are we as sheep to know the difference? We need the discernment that can only come from time in God's word. We must first know the voice of Jesus, our good shepherd. If someone speaks words in opposition to Jesus's words, then we don't follow. If a spiritual leader tells you to do something that Scripture tells you not to do, run the other way.

In contrast, godly leaders tell us hard things that are for our good, in accordance to God's word. We may not like what they say when their teaching shines light on sinful patterns in our lives. But we need to listen to them. They speak the truth, and they speak it in love, wanting us to walk by the Spirit, not by the flesh (Gal. 5:13–26).

You may be wondering: *What does a godly leader look like?* and *What are the types of leaders we have in the church?* Paul wrote a description to Timothy, explaining two leadership roles in the church—overseers (often called elders) and deacons:

> Therefore an overseer must be above reproach, the husband of one wife, sober-minded, self-controlled, respectable, hospitable, able to teach, not a drunkard, not violent but gentle, not quarrelsome, not a lover of money. . . . Deacons likewise must be dignified, not double-tongued, not addicted to much wine, not greedy for dishonest gain. (1 Tim. 3:2–8)

Notice some of these characteristics: self-controlled, gentle, not a lover of money, not addicted to much wine, not greedy. These leaders are to be above reproach. We're not to follow just any person who comes along. We're to look at both their doctrine (what they believe about God) and their lives. These are the leaders we follow, listen to, and seek to encourage in their work. They serve us by their labors, and we serve them by our prayers. We need their accountability and authority in our lives.

Fellowship and Care

Last December my friend Lauren called. I could hear the panic in her voice as soon as I picked up the phone. She was pregnant with twins, so I thought she might be rushing to the hospital for an early delivery. I knew her husband, Joel, was heading out of town that day, so I wondered if she might need some help. However, she wasn't at the hospital; she was at the pediatrician's with her other two children, four-year-old Caroline and two-year-old Jennings. She'd taken Jennings to the doctor because he'd been sick for the past couple of months and just wasn't getting better. The doctor decided to run some extra blood tests and came back with shocking and terrible news: "Jennings has leukemia."

Jennings was immediately admitted to the children's hospital and began chemo the next day. He wouldn't leave the hospital for six weeks.

Did I mention Lauren was also pregnant with twins and had a four-year old daughter? Three weeks after Jennings started treatment, Lauren switched hospital floors to give birth to two healthy twins. In the meantime, as tests came back, the doctors informed them that Jennings had a rare form of leukemia. It was more difficult to treat and required a move to Memphis for a bone marrow transplant.

It was unimaginable: a move to Memphis, with four children under four, one battling a life-threatening illness that required constant care.

The burden they were given simply couldn't be carried on their own. Within twenty-four hours of the initial diagnosis, a group of fifteen church members gathered in my living room. Over the next two hours we discussed every type of physical-care item we could think of and divided up tasks, from taking the family's trash to the street to organizing meals, both at the hospital and at home. Each person at that meeting played a vital role in the mountain of physical needs that would pile up over the next six months. We couldn't heal Jennings, but we could help his family.

When they moved to Memphis, the church there—people whom Lauren and Joel had never met—brought meals, took their daughter to the pool, prayed, and visited, offering to do anything they could to help. In the midst of so many terrible moments, the church (both in Charlotte and in Memphis) surrounded this family. We couldn't rescue them, we couldn't answer the *why* questions, we couldn't cure cancer, but we could be there, walking with them in the trial.

I don't know how people survive without the church. And it's not just in the life-changing moments, like my friend Lauren faced. It's in the everyday moments of life. I need people to remind me of the truth and help me walk in it. I need friends to rejoice with me when I'm rejoicing and mourn with me when I'm mourning. I need to be with them worshiping God every week. We can't do this life on our own. Yet so many of us try.

Hebrews tells us, "Let us consider how to stir up one another to love and good works, not neglecting to meet together, as is the habit of some, but encouraging one another, and all the more as you see the Day drawing near" (Heb. 10:24–25). The fellowship and care we have to offer one another is different from any other social group, club, or committee. Collectively, we're a body of people waiting together, looking forward to Christ's return. The church is a little taste of home in the midst of our journey through a foreign land. Don't miss it. It's not perfect, but it's family.

Mission and Ministry

The church isn't just a group of friends waiting it out until Jesus returns. We're people on a mission. There's an entire world out there of people who don't know the good news. As individuals, we can only do so much. But as the church, we can go throughout the world sharing Jesus. For you, that might mean loving a little child all day or working in a law firm and befriending your coworkers. Your job may allow you to support the woman who moves across the world to share Jesus with a woman who has never heard his name. One person may spend years learning Greek to teach the church, while another may move near a soup kitchen to serve the poor. Both are serving Jesus. Both need each other, "for as in one body we have many members, and the members do not all have the same function, so we, though many, are one body in Christ, and individually members one of another" (Rom. 12:4–5). We're not in competition with one another; rather, our different roles complete what is lacking in the other. Alone, I can be only one part of the body. As the church, we can do so much more together than we can do on our own.

Wandering in Unbelief

We need the church, and the church needs us. Yet we often find ourselves worn and weary when it comes to the church. Frustrations mount, and unmet expectations build walls of bitterness. It's easy to listen to lies about the church and wander from it. What are some of the lies that we hear and listen to? Let's consider three common lies.

Lie 1: "God Doesn't Care If I Go to Church"

It's tempting to believe that the church is unimportant. All that really matters is our connection to God. If we're "all good" with God, then what difference does it make if we go to church? Can't we worship God anywhere since he is everywhere?

For those in the West, used to an individualistic mindset, it's tempting to believe that the only relationship God cares about is the vertical one. If we pray and read the Bible, isn't that enough? Well, the answer is no. God's love for us is manifested as we love one another. God calls people to himself and unites them to Christ. We aren't individual members, but we belong to one another. As we love one another, we proclaim God's great love. God cares greatly that you are a part of a church. It's part of his good provision and plan for you.

Lie 2: "I'm Too Busy to Go to Church"

Here's the truth: we prioritize what we believe makes a difference. If you believe it matters that your family eats all organic food, you'll spend considerable time and effort making sure that happens. If you believe exercise is important, you'll find time to work out. If you believe friendships are valuable, you'll make time for your friends.

If you believe church matters, you'll make it a priority. You'll forgo traveling every weekend for vacation trips. You'll bring your children even though it doesn't work for their nap schedule. You'll get to bed earlier on Saturday night (even though friends are staying out late) so you can be at church on Sunday morning. And you won't be there only for service; you'll carve out time in your week to build relationships with other church members. You'll make the choice to actively commit rather than passively attend. An overly busy schedule is not the problem keeping you from church. Our beliefs drive our actions and what we choose to prioritize. Choose the church.

Lie 3: "I've Been Hurt by the Church"

Let me say clearly that there are many unhealthy churches, and there's no perfect church. Some churches hurt their members by failures in leadership, false teaching, and wrong priorities. Please don't commit unwaveringly to a church regardless of what it believes or how the leadership acts. Don't remain in a church that is unbiblical or sinful in its application of truth. Use spiritual discernment and seek the wisdom of others.

However, don't give up on the church as a whole just because you've been a part of an unhealthy one. As Jackie Hill Perry wisely tweeted, "Do you know who God used to heal me of my church hurt? The church."[10] Hannah Anderson added these insights: "The discernment that equips us to see God's goodness in the world despite its brokenness is the same discernment that equips us to see God's goodness in the church despite her brokenness."

The church isn't perfect. There are wolves among us, seeking to destroy the flock (Acts 20:29). It's full of saints struggling with sin. Yet it's God's home for his people while they journey together. I know you may be afraid of not fitting in or being hurt again, but you need the people of God. Keep going. Keep pursuing. Keep praying. May God put you in a church to heal the hurt you've experienced.

Walking by Faith: Good News for Grace-Filled Living

We're not saved by our church attendance, but church is a vital part of life as one who has been saved. As we abide in Christ, we're connected to one another. If one part suffers, we all suffer. If one part rejoices, we all experience the joy. Christ's fullness unifies us with one another.

Paul wrote most of his letters to churches rather than to individuals. He exhorted, "Strive to excel in building up the church" (1 Cor.14:12). We seek to excel at many things—our jobs, our marriages, our homes, our parenting. How can we strive to build up the church? It will look different for each of us, but it will involve self-sacrifice and effort.

Some serve faithfully in the church nursery for years. Others set up chairs and welcome new people. Some help care for the poor or lead an outreach Bible study. God has uniquely gifted each person to serve the body. The type of service is less important than the heart of service. We don't labor to build up the church to earn God's favor. We build up the church because we are favored. God's grace upon us allows us to pour out grace on others. We love one another because he first loved us.

The church is your home away from home. You need the church, and the church needs you. We love the church not because it's perfect but because Christ loves the church—she's his bride. Today she may not be lovely, but one day she will be resplendent (Rev. 21:2).

Before You Meet: Practical Tools to Help You Grow

Oftentimes we are unaware of all that's going on at the church we attend. I encourage you to visit your church's website and read over its mission statement, identify its ministry partners and the missionaries they support, and learn about the staff team. Take a few minutes to read through the staff list and pray for the leaders of your church, that God would encourage and sustain them in their work.[11]

Prayerfully consider the ways you can grow in your commitment to the local church as you discuss the following questions.

While You Meet: Questions for Discussion

1. Did you grow up in the church? If so, was it a positive or negative experience? How so?

2. How would you describe yourself: church wounded, church fatigued, church dissatisfied, or church healthy?

3. What role has the church played in your spiritual growth?

4. How are you currently serving in the church? In what ways would you like to use your gifts in the church?

5. Are you a member of your church? Why or why not? How would you describe your church attendance?

6. Which of the three lies about church keep you from going deeper with your church community? Which of these do you struggle with most?

7. In what ways have you experienced fellowship and care from a church? How did that impact you?

Until You Meet Again: Growing in Godliness

Based on your discussion, consider one area in which you'd like to make a change before you meet next time. It could be to start doing something that will help you grow spiritually or to stop doing something that is preventing your growth. Write it in the space below and discuss it the next time you meet.

5

It's Good News!

Sharing Your Faith with Others

Coming to faith in Jesus is like coming home to a place we have always wanted but never knew we desired. . . . Each time we share the gospel with students, friends, coworkers, or family members, we are giving them a chance to finally come home.

—*SharDavia Walker*

Gardening is one of my favorite hobbies. My husband always chuckles at my wide-eyed amazement when I gather tomatoes and peppers from the garden and come in proclaiming, "Look at these beautiful tomatoes!" The delight of watching something grow—and then enjoy eating it—hasn't gotten old after years of gardening.

In turn, my husband loves to fish. Every summer, as soon as we get to the beach, he's got his pole out and ready, eager to hook the bait. Every time the line jiggles with a new catch, he runs excitedly to the water, ready to reel in whatever he's hooked. He's caught stingrays, sharks, and a variety of fish we enjoy eating for dinner: blue fish, seabass, and Spanish mackerel. Whatever the catch, the joy of reeling something in never gets old.

Interestingly, both fishing and sowing were images Jesus used to describe evangelism. He promised his disciples, "Follow me, and I will make you fishers of men" (Matt 4:19). In addition, Jesus taught the parable of the sower to explain the different types of reactions to the gospel message (Luke 8). He told his disciples, "Look, I tell you, lift up your eyes, and see that the fields are white for harvest" (John 4:35).

When I work in my garden or watch my husband fish, I often meditate on Jesus's words. The joy of an earthly garden or a fresh catch are echoes of a greater harvest, a better feast. As God's people, we're invited to participate in sowing seeds of faith as we share the gospel message with others. I can often feel fearful or unprepared or think I need a seminary degree to share about God, but the message of the gospel is simple. Just as a child can learn to plant seeds or cast a net, we can all learn to share our faith.

Wisdom for Life

Just before his ascension, Jesus gave the disciples their marching orders for what to do after his departure:

> Jesus came and said to them, "All authority in heaven and on earth has been given to me. Go therefore and make disciples of all nations, baptizing them in the name of the Father and of the Son and of the Holy Spirit, teaching them to observe all that I have commanded you. And behold, I am with you always, to the end of the age." (Matt. 28:17–20)

With heavenly authority Jesus sends his people on an earthly mission. We're to go into all the world and make disciples, baptizing them in the name of our Trinitarian God: Father, Son, and Holy Spirit. We teach them to obey his commands. We do so with confidence, because Jesus is with us always and has overcome the world and the dominion of darkness.

You may read these words and feel unprepared or ill-equipped to teach others about God. It's easy to believe that disciple making should be left to trained professionals. However, Jesus's disciples weren't trained theologians—most of them were uneducated, common men (Acts 4:13). The message goes forth not by our eloquence or persuasion but by the Spirit's power. In fact, our weaknesses, our fears, our bumbling attempts, and our stammering speech may be the way the power of the Spirit is demonstrated (1 Cor. 2:1–4). Thankfully, we don't rest on the power of our argument but on the power of our God. He is with us.

The simplicity of the message is summed up in the familiar words of John 3:16. However, it's important not to neglect verses 17 and 18:

> For God so loved the world, that he gave his only Son, that whoever believes in him should not perish but have eternal life. For God did not send his Son into the world to condemn the world, but in order that the world might be saved through him. Whoever believes in him is not condemned, but whoever does not believe is condemned already, because he has not believed in the name of the only Son of God. (John 3:16–18)

The best news the world has ever received is the message of the gospel. We were dead in our sins (Eph. 2:1), unable to make ourselves alive, held captive by sin, and destined for destruction. Because of his great love for us, God sent his Son to rescue and redeem us.

What was his rescue plan? Jesus lived a perfect life so that he could be the perfect sacrifice. At the cross, God's love and holiness meet in a spectacular display of his character. God's perfect justice and righteousness required that every sin be paid in full. In love and mercy, Jesus let all the payment for our debt fall on himself. He took the punishment so that we might be free from sin's penalty and power. The cross acts as a divine sponge, soaking up the righteous wrath of God so that there is none left for all who call on the name of Jesus for salvation.

I'm always looking for a good deal, and the gospel beats any BOGO offer the world has ever seen. However, with the good news, we also find the bad news: whoever does not believe in Jesus is condemned. This truth fuels our evangelism. There are many who have never heard the good news. They may look like their lives are just fine, but they are moments from destruction.

Some time ago, Hurricane Florence pounded the North Carolina coast. The week beforehand, we watched as Florence made her advance. Knowing she was heading our way led to mandatory evacuations for all of eastern North Carolina. Even though we were far inland, reports showed that Charlotte would receive record rainfalls that could lead to devastating floods.

The day before Hurricane Florence hit Charlotte, the weather was lovely. Had I not known a hurricane was coming, I would have simply thought the increasing winds were a welcome relief from the heat and humidity. If the weather reports hadn't warned us, we might have been unprepared for the flooding and power outages that plagued our city.

Evangelism is God's warning system for the coming storm. God sees the injustice, the devastation, the abuse, and the suffering of our world, and he is coming to repay every evil that has ever occurred. We can either face his judgment by our own merits or flee to Jesus and take refuge in him, hiding in the shelter of his righteousness. There is no other option. Either we will pay for our sins for eternity, or Jesus will pay our debt.

When the hurricane was heading our way, it was all we talked about. Friends told friends which stores still had water and where to find bread. We made arrangements in case the power went out. My husband built a drainage system to keep our creek from overflowing. We worked together to make sure everyone had what they needed to endure the storm.

Many don't know to seek refuge because today the sun is shining. They don't know to prepare because they are unaware of their predicament. Through evangelism, we call out to our friends and neighbors warning them and helping them find refuge in Jesus. It's the ultimate way we fulfill the command to love our neighbor as ourselves. The greatest unkindness is to leave people in their sin when the ransom for their release has already been paid in full.

Even with the good news before us and the sobering truth to motivate us, evangelizing so often feels uncomfortable. Many of us have been taught that polite conversation never involves religion or politics. In our postmodern era, who are we to tell anyone what they should believe or how they should behave?

Wandering in Unbelief

Whispers of unbelief tend to plague us when we contemplate sharing our faith. Our fears can paralyze our attempts to scatter seed and cast nets. Following are a few fears I have to fight against when it comes to evangelism.

Fear 1: "I'm Not Good at Sharing My Faith"

My husband is one of the best evangelists I've ever seen. Years ago we participated in an evangelism café at a church. One traveler who was waiting for a train wandered in, and my husband engaged him in spiritual conversation. As they discussed a variety of topics, my husband handled each question with grace and truth. He adeptly engaged and challenged the man's worldview, hoping not just to defend Christianity but to show him it was the only viable option.

I watched him with wonder, and all my insecurities rose to the surface: *I could never do that. I'm not equipped well enough to share my faith.* Do you ever feel that too? We look at experts and decide it's best to leave evangelism to them. However, this is when we need to do battle in our own mind. Our job is to scatter the seed and throw the net. We can't ensure the seed will grow or that we'll find fish in the net. Yes, we can study and improve our techniques, but we'll never learn if we don't try. As for those questions someone asks you that you find difficult to answer, ask for help from a pastor or ministry leader. Search the web for answers. Read a book. When we find ourselves with a lack of words to explain, the Lord can use those instances to grow our own faith.

My husband didn't become a good evangelist by going to seminary. He learned in the school of experience. Every Friday night in college he went out on the main street of our campus and did evangelism. Those evenings of talking to strangers (and sometimes not knowing what to say) developed his ability to talk about his faith with others. If we want to learn, one of the best training grounds is to start today. Who in your life can you share your faith with today? You don't have to have all the answers. Tell your story of mercy and grace and pray expectantly for the Lord to grow the seeds you scatter.

Fear 2: "It Will Be Uncomfortable"

Last spring I was sitting alone at a hotel having breakfast when one of the chefs walked by and started talking to me. He asked me what I did for a living, and when I told him I work for my church, our casual conversation detoured into spiritual matters. He made multiple statements that I disagreed with: *All religions are really the same. It's just about being a good person. It doesn't matter if you go to church.*

As he made these statements, I sat there with a blank look on my face. Here was an opening to share the good news, and I felt unsure how to kindly respond to his belief system without making our pleasant conversation uncomfortable. My desire to be nice and friendly overpowered my desire to share my faith. And in doing so, I failed to love—truly love—the person in front of me who wanted to engage in a spiritual conversation. He was confident to share his truth claims with me, but I was fearful and reticent to challenge his confident assertions.

I allowed my fear of a brief moment of discomfort to prevent me from sharing eternal joyful truths. I tried to bumble my way through my thoughts with him, but I failed to be truly bold. Why? I had nothing to lose, and he potentially had everything to gain. Let me encourage you (and myself)—don't let fear of discomfort prevent you from the joy that evangelism can bring. If we never boldly throw the net, we'll never get to experience the thrill of the catch.

Fear 3: "I May Lose a Friend"

While we may be reticent to experience the discomfort of sharing our faith with someone we don't know, we can be downright terrified of sharing our faith with those we love. Our fear of losing the relationship, causing an argument, or coming across as "holier than thou" often prevents us from telling others the good news. It's even more complicated in places like the South where everyone is supposedly a Christian, yet many lives seem untouched by the Spirit-filled presence of Jesus.

When these fears surface, it's helpful to remind ourselves of the truth of our loved one's predicament. They're not okay without Jesus. I once read the story of two men trapped in a tiny concrete outpost building when flood waters began to rise. They were unable to escape and would have died except for the unrelenting courage of a friend who eventually helped break a window from the outside. He worked tirelessly trying to find a solution, knowing that every minute counted. When the water was almost to the ceiling, he finally pounded out the window, allowing them to swim free.

Our mission is similar to this friendly rescuer. While we don't want to pound the gospel into those we love, we do want to continue in every way possible to share the good news with those we love. We want to be creative and look for new ways to share, because we know the dire nature of their predicament. They're trapped in their sin and need the freedom that only the gospel can offer. May we be bold in our love, faithful in prayer, and steadfast in our pursuit until they are released from the prison of unbelief.

Walking by Faith: Good News for Grace-Filled Living

Everyone's life is different. There's no one-size-fits-all approach to evangelism. However, I've found a few ways to share my faith that have fit a variety of seasons of life. As we walk by faith, by God's grace, we can grow to be people who joyfully share the good news.

Be on the Lookout

I once heard a missionary share his simple method for evangelism:

- pray for opportunities
- meet people
- share the gospel
- pray that the Spirit would work in their hearts

It's a wonderfully simple way to live an evangelistic life, isn't it? What if we lived each day with that as our to-do list? Perhaps if we began our day praying for opportunities to share our faith—at work, with a neighbor, at the grocery store—we'd have better vision to see when these opportunities arise.

Maybe that unwanted trip to the doctor's office is more than just an inconvenience in your day. Perhaps the waiting room is your mission field today. Maybe that baseball team your child plays on isn't just about him becoming the most amazing pitcher. Perhaps there's another family on the team that needs the hope of Jesus. Maybe that difficult work assignment is exactly where the Lord is sending you today. Perhaps those long hours will give you opportunity to share with someone who is hurting and lost.

Ask the Spirit to give you eyes to see. May we look and see the fields that are white for harvest. Wherever you go today, be on the lookout for opportunities to share. And pray. There's nothing that prepares our heart more than prayer, and our message—no matter how eloquent—is only fumbling words without the Spirit's power. As J. I. Packer said:

> God will make us pray before he blesses our labors in order that we may constantly learn afresh that we depend on God for everything. And then, when God permits us to see conversions, we shall not be tempted to ascribe them to our own gifts, or skill, or wisdom, or persuasiveness, but to his work alone, and so we shall know whom we ought to thank for them.[12]

Build Relationships

One of the simple ways we till the soil for our evangelistic efforts is by building relationships with others. When we love others, in both word and deed, the beauty of Christ adorns our gospel message. Get to know people, listen to their stories, weep when they weep, rejoice when they rejoice. Love others as Christ first loved you. As Paul wrote of his ministry among the Thessalonians, "But we were gentle among you, like a nursing mother taking care of her own children. So, being affectionately desirous of you, we were ready to share with you not only the gospel of God but also our own selves, because you had become very dear to us" (1 Thess. 2:7–8).

Because we are limited, we can't build deep relationships with everyone. So it's good to consider one or two specific people in whom we can invest with our prayers, time, and energy. As you consider the unbelievers in your life, who among them do you naturally enjoy spending time with?

When I was in college, I was involved in a ministry that encouraged us to pray for two specific people over the course of the upcoming year. I was in a large sorority, so this helped me focus my attention and time. I prayed for two women, got to know them, listened to their stories, and tried to be a friend. It didn't restrict me from sharing with others, but it helped me to be purposeful and thoughtful in my friendship.

Be Yourself

It seems odd to say this, but one of the easiest ways we can share the gospel is simply to share honestly with others about our lives. When we're heading out for the evening, we can tell our neighbor, "Oh, I'm going to a meeting," or we can tell them a little more, "Oh, I'm going to this great Bible study. Let me know if you'd ever like to come along. It's such a wonderful group of women." Sharing a small glimpse into your life may serve as an opportunity for your neighbor to come and hear the gospel. And all you did was share your evening plans.

Sometimes, as believers, we forget how lonely most people are. We're more digitally connected than ever, but increasingly many people have few opportunities to build relationships with real people. Life in the church is an invitation to a community that many people have never experienced. Sharing your faith can begin with the simple act of inviting a friend to your church, Bible study, or small-group social. Also, don't feel like you have to be perfect. Sharing all parts of your life—including your mistakes and failures—can help others understand that Christianity isn't for perfect people but for sinners who need a Savior.

Start a Bible Study

Years ago, a group of us decided to start a Bible study at our children's preschool. As we formed the group, we hoped to create a place where women who'd never studied the Bible would feel comfortable coming and learning about Christianity. Instead, our initial Bible study was mainly ladies from church who shared our evangelistic hopes. In retrospect, I realize the Lord was building our community in those first two years so that we'd have a loving place to invite other moms. He gave us a community so that we could share it with others. Eventually he brought the women we were hoping to reach.

We began sending an invitation to each woman in our preschool for a back-to-school brunch to introduce ourselves and tell them about Bible study. I was always surprised by who decided to come, but each year we had a few who would join the group. Then week after week, month after month, year after year, we studied the Bible together.

Over many years of leading outreach studies, I've become convinced that the Bible is the most powerful tool we have in evangelism. God uses his word to fashion hearts and transform minds. It's living and active. We see Jesus in all his complexity. As we study, honest discussions of struggles and heartache are bathed in the hope of the gospel as the word becomes the center of relationships. His word, discussed and mulled over among a group of women, changes lives.

I encourage you to be on the lookout, build relationships, be yourself, and share God's word with the lost. A fisherman cannot make a fish bite, nor can a farmer make a seed grow. They can increase in wisdom and understanding as they perform their tasks, but they must wait in hope for the results. Similarly, we entrust all our evangelistic efforts to the Lord. We're not held accountable for the souls we're trying to reach but for our obedience to Christ's call to "go and make disciples" (Matt. 28:19).

Nevertheless, the excitement of catching a fish or watching a plant grow greatly encourages the laborer in her task. I'm so thankful the Lord has allowed me to see lives changed. I have the same hope for each of us to prayerfully live by Jesus's words: "The harvest is plentiful, but the workers are few. Ask the Lord of the harvest, therefore, to send out workers to his harvest field" (Luke 10:2).

Before You Meet: Practical Tools to Help You Grow

Take a few minutes to look at a visual tool from the Navigators called "One-Verse Evangelism: How to Share Christ's Love Conversationally and Visually."[13] Have you seen this bridge diagram before? How is it helpful as you think about sharing your faith?

Identify two people in your life for whom you will pray for opportunities to share the gospel in the year to come.

While You Meet: Questions for Discussion

1. How did you first hear the message of the gospel? How did other people share their faith with you?

2. In what ways have you shared your faith with others?

3. What keeps you from sharing your faith with others? Did you resonate with any of the fears: I'm not good at sharing my faith, it's uncomfortable, or I'm fearful of losing a friend? Which one in particular stood out to you as a struggle?

4. In what ways could you be on the lookout for opportunities to share the gospel as you go about your day? Consider the past week. Can you think of any situations in which you could have shared your faith (even in a small way) with someone else?

5. In the next week, what steps can you take to share your faith with one other person? How about during the next month? It can be as simple as inviting someone to go to church with you or as bold as asking someone you know is not a Christian to study the Bible with you for two months.

6. Take some time to pray together for the lost in your lives. And pray for one another that you may have boldness to share the good news with others (Eph. 6:20).

Until You Meet Again: Growing in Godliness

Based on your discussion, consider one area in which you'd like to make a change before you meet next time. It could be to start doing something that will help you grow spiritually or to stop doing something that is preventing your growth. Write it in the space below and discuss it the next time you meet.

6

Prayer

Pouring Out Your Heart to God

It is no small thing that we can use the word Abba as we cry out to our Father. . . . It is a grace to us that we can cry out to the Lord in prayer in such intimate and personal ways. He gives us that access.

—*Trillia Newbell*

Falling in love is a pretty time-consuming endeavor. When those first flutters of attraction take flight, there's an equal desire to know and be known. Conversations extend late into the night, work is set aside, and time together is found in the busiest of schedules. Even as relationships mature and move past the early stages of infatuation (which is somewhat needed for society to properly function), one of the most important parts of any relationship is communication.

I may not be in the early stages of my romance with my husband, but he's still the one I want to talk to about my day, whether it's struggles at work or the hilarious comment our daughter made at lunch. I want to share with him about the hard, rejoice with him about the good, mourn our losses, and celebrate our joys. I want to tell him about everything because I love him.

Whether it's your best friend, your mom, your sister, your co-worker, your roommate, or your spouse that you talk to most, we build relationships by sharing our lives with one another. While various friendships may ebb and flow by distance, distrust, or death, there's one relationship we can invest in that promises to last. This assurance can only come from God himself: "For I am sure that neither death nor life, nor angels nor rulers, nor things present nor things to come, nor powers, nor height nor depth, nor anything else in all creation, will be able to separate us from the love of God in Christ Jesus our Lord" (Rom. 8:38–39).

Our relationship with God is built on a solid, eternal foundation. We grow this relationship much like we build a friendship with anyone else. We spend time together. God speaks to us through his word, and we speak to God through prayer. Prayer requires time and stillness—two things that are rare commodities in our always-connected, always-available, smartphone society.

It's difficult to build a habit of prayer, but we need it—oh, how much we need it! To remind ourselves of the importance of prayer, we'll explore the wisdom the Bible offers us on prayer, consider why we wander from this habit, and think through practical ways to grow our prayer lives. If your prayer life isn't what you want it to be, there's good news: you can start today building new habits and life-giving patterns for spiritual refreshment.

Wisdom for Life

Prayer permeates the Scriptures. Old Testament saints called out to God in their distress and joyfully praised him in song. Paul, James, Peter, John, and Jude shared their prayers and encouraged prayerfulness in their letters to the churches. Jesus taught of prayer by both his example and his instruction. Prayer is part of the Christian life. God wants more than outward conformity to his laws—he wants our hearts. So he invites us to pray.

There's so much we could say about prayer. In fact, many full-sized books have been written on this topic. To help us get a general sense of prayer, let's consider the who, what, when, why, and how that the Bible teaches us about prayer.

Who?

Peter wrote that the Lord hears the prayer of the righteous but that his face is against those who do evil (1 Pet. 3:12). We may read a passage like that and conclude that before we pray, we've got to work hard and make ourselves right enough to go into God's presence. That's bad news for us—we can never get ourselves right enough to go before God. However, there's good news: if we're in Christ, Scripture tells us that we're counted as righteous (Rom. 5:19). We can boldly go into the presence of God and seek his help, knowing that he listens to us not because of our righteousness but because of Christ's perfect righteousness, given to us. God accepts us in his presence and hears us as his beloved children.

My husband serves as president of a seminary, which can make some students feel somewhat intimidated to go in his office to ask him a simple question. One student told me that she practiced exactly what she was going to say before she entered because she was so nervous (thankfully, she survived to tell me about it).

About a week later, I dropped by my husband's office with our children, after running an errand, just to say hello. The three of them boldly bounded into his office, rushing around the room, spinning in his office chair with delight, laughing at each other as they tried on his robe. They felt no such intimidation or need to perform in his presence. They didn't see my husband as an intimidating seminary professor. They know him as their dad, who delights in their laughter and welcomes them with hugs.

That's the loving picture I want you to have as you go to the Lord in prayer. I know many people have complicated relationships with their earthly fathers or other authorities that can make approaching God a fearful thing. But the Scriptures invite us to enter with confidence because of Jesus: "Let us then with confidence draw near to the throne of grace, that we may receive mercy and find grace to help in time of need" (Heb. 4:16). It's a privilege to be able to draw near. Don't be shackled by fear and miss the freedom you have. He loves you. He listens to you. He delights in you. Enter into his presence with joy.

What?

The Scriptures invite us to pray for a variety of needs. Hannah called out to God in distress because of infertility (1 Sam. 1:10). The psalmist cried out to God with his tears (Ps. 39:12). James told us to ask God for wisdom (James 1:5) and join with the elders to pray for healing (James 5:14). Paul told the Philippians to take their anxieties to God in prayer (Phil. 4:6), and he prayed that they might grow in love for God and in spiritual discernment (Phil. 1:9). He also told us to pray even when we're not sure what to pray because the Spirit will intercede on our behalf (Rom. 8:26).

Jesus taught his disciples to pray so that they wouldn't enter into temptation (Mark 14:38). He commanded us to love our enemies and pray for those who persecute us (Matt. 5:44). Most of all, he gave us the Lord's Prayer, showing us how to pray for God's glory, our daily bread, and the forgiveness we desperately need (Matt. 6:9–13).

Savor this good news: you don't have to handle life's burdens on your own. What weighs anxiously on your heart today? Take it to the Lord in prayer. What situation seems impossible to change? Take it to the Lord in prayer. Who seems beyond the hope of the gospel? Take them to the Lord in prayer. How would you like to grow to be more like Jesus? Take it to the Lord in prayer.

It's so easy to allow our thoughts to consume our mind with worry. There is freedom when we take our concerns to the Lord.

Why?

We pray because God hears us, but we also pray because God is able to do what we cannot. We're unable to see or even imagine the ways he might work, because we're finite, limited beings. Ephesians tells us that God is "able to do far more abundantly than all that we ask or think" (Eph. 3:20). When we pray, we are asking the infinite God of all the universe for help. He knows all. He sees all. He is all-powerful. He's our greatest hope, and we can pour out our burdens to him. It's the height of pride not to pray. Humility—a right understanding of ourselves—brings us to our knees asking for help. We pray because we're not God. We can't change minds, circumstances, or hearts. Only God can.

When?

Prayer is to be a daily habit of our lives. The early disciples devoted themselves to prayer (Acts 1:14). Paul instructed the Romans to be constant in prayer (Rom. 12:12), the Ephesians to pray at all times (Eph. 6:18), and the Colossians to continue steadfastly in prayer (Col. 4:2). Prayer isn't just one moment (although it is good to set aside specific times for prayer), but a conversation that goes throughout our day. We can pray immediately at any time and in any place, asking God to be at work.

How?

Jesus cares how we pray. He instructed his disciples not to heap up empty phrases in an attempt to sound good (Matt. 6:7), nor to pray to be seen by others (Matt. 6:5). We're to go into our rooms, shut the door, and pray in secret (Matt. 6:6).

Jesus's instruction to pray in secret doesn't mean that it's wrong to pray with others. Jesus took Peter, John, and James up to the mountain to pray. However, we're warned against having a prayer life that is more about outward impressions than inward relationship. We need to pray with one another, and we need to pray alone. Jesus modeled the importance of both.

Wandering in Unbelief

It's easy to believe in the power and necessity of prayer but difficult to live out what we believe. Often in the busyness of life, we become so consumed with the doing that we miss time alone on our knees before God. We also may grow discouraged when it seems that our prayers have little effect. Following are four reasons we sometimes drift from a life of prayer.

Reason 1: "I'm Too Busy"

Most of us feel quickly consumed by the various expectations of our day that pile up like laundry waiting to be folded. It's easy to go from our morning coffee into our day without stopping to check the morning news, much less be still and pray.

While we may be reticent to admit it, how we spend our time exposes what we really believe. If we truly believe that prayer matters—that God providentially uses our prayers to accomplish his good purposes—then we'd take the time to be still before the Lord in prayer. However, often we live in the false understanding that our hard work is the key to our success, that we can shape our circumstances by our own efforts, and that at the end of the day, we're in charge of our own lives. This mistaken belief keeps us from prayer.

We can fight the lie of "I'm too busy to pray" by replacing it with the truth that our busyness is the exact reason we need prayer. Often we really do have too much to do. We're not able to do it all on our own. Prayer helps us to release the urgent expectations of others into the capable hands of our ever-present God. We can look at all that needs to be done and ask God to do more than we can even imagine. In the mystery of his providence, he can shape the course of our days in ways that we may not expect. He can clear our schedule and arrange our paths in ways that may surprise us. He can also strengthen us for the tasks at hand in ways that are beyond our abilities. He uses our prayers to accomplish—through our dependence on him—what is impossible in our own strength.

Prayer acts as a pause to the demands of our day. By sitting before the Lord and prayerfully entrusting our schedules to him, we may find we clearly discern the places we need to say no, as well as the places we can sacrificially say yes, trusting God's power to be at work in us and through us.

Yes, we are busy people. That's the exact reason we must be praying people.

Reason 2: "It's More Important to Do Something"

It's not just a busy day that keeps us from prayer; it's also our desire to do something practical to help those we love. It's a right and good desire to come alongside people and help however we can serve them. Yet we often forget that prayer is an essential part of the way we lovingly serve others.

In the midst of so many things we can *see* that need to be done, it's difficult to choose the *unseen* work of prayer. While people may appreciate our labors of bringing a meal or helping with their children, they may never know the months or years we spent praying on their behalf. The visible nature of some service acts as a natural reward—people are rightly thankful! The unseen nature of prayer means we trust that the Lord sees our labors and that he will reward our secret service to others (Matt. 6:6).

Our prayer life isn't in opposition to serving others in tangible ways. I've actually found the complete opposite to be true. A rich prayer life fuels and empowers our service to others. As we put prayer first, the Lord will move and direct us in faithful love to the hurting, needy, and doubting. We can let go of having to do it all, because we've prayed to the God who is Lord of all. Setting first things first does not diminish our service; rather, it supernaturally increases our labors as God works in ways that cause us to over-flow with praise.

Reason 3: "I'm Easily Distracted"

Let's face it: prayer is hard work. My mind wanders, forgotten tasks are remembered, and suddenly all the dust on my side table needs to be dealt with right away. Everything in me wants to check my phone to make sure I didn't miss something important. It's hard to be still when I'm energized and ready to get going with my day.

Sometimes we may look at how easily distracted we can become and think to ourselves, *I'm just not very good at prayer. I'll leave it up to the ones who are naturally good at it.* However, prayer is like any language; we become fluent in it the more we practice it. The more we allow time to talk to God, the more we'll find ourselves talking to him throughout the day. Prayer is a learned response to the Spirit at work in our hearts. This is why Jesus taught his disciples how to pray—it doesn't just happen naturally.

Our prayer life is something that grows as we walk with God, day to day, year to year. If yours isn't where you'd like it to be today, that's okay (mine isn't either!). However, there are habits and helpful means by which God can grow our enjoyment of prayer.

Reason 4: "It's Not Working"

Sometimes we've prayed so long for something but our praying seems to have no effect, so we give up. I've prayed for healing that ended in death, for wombs that never opened, for spouses that never appeared, and for prodigals that still remain far from home. We may never understand on this side of eternity the reasons God answers no when we so desperately long for a yes. It's tempting to believe the lie that a yes from God confirms his blessing, while a no is a form of punishment or heavenly disapproval. Sometimes we wonder if he even hears our desperate cries. However, God's no to our prayers is always a yes to his providential purposes. He's at work in ways we may not understand. It's difficult, but by faith we keep praying. Don't give up and don't lose heart. He sees you. He loves you. He hears you.

Walking by Faith: Good News for Grace-Filled Living

At some point when I was a teenager, an older believer taught me the acronym ACTS to help me pray. It simply stands for Adoration, Confession, Thanksgiving, and Supplication. It helped me learn a pattern of prayer that encouraged me to focus on the Lord's goodness, consider my sin and need for forgiveness, offer up thanksgiving, and present my requests to God.

There are a variety of different tools we can use to help us in the content of our prayers and to keep us focused during our prayer time. I'll share a few ways that I've learned to pray throughout the years, but these are just suggestions that have helped me. To continue to grow your own prayer life, I also encourage you to talk to your mentor or friends about ways they've strengthened their prayer life and what has helped them.

Prayer Journal

When I was fifteen years old, the devotional book I was using encouraged the practice of journaling for a week. Since I wasn't really sure what to write about, I decided to simply begin writing a letter to God each day. That one week of journaling turned into thirty years—I'm now forty-five, and I'm still writing a letter to God each day. I have boxes of prayer journals stored in my attic that consist of years and years of pouring my heart out to God.

Writing out my prayers has helped me in a few ways. It keeps my mind focused and fully engaged. It helps me pray specifically and purposefully. I've also had the benefit of seeing specific prayer requests answered (sometimes the very day I prayed them!). When I've been hurt by someone, I've found that writing out my frustrations and anger has helped me slow down and gain perspective. It's also allowed me to see more clearly when I need to repent and ask forgiveness.

Most importantly, writing out my prayers has grown my friendship with God. When I write, Scripture comes to mind, encouraging me, convicting me, comforting me. It's a back-and-forth conversation with God that happens as writing slows me down. It has helped me understand more fully that prayer isn't just putting forth our requests to God—it's an act of walking with him, talking with him, interacting with him, and knowing him.

While writing out prayers isn't for everyone, it might be something to try for a week. Who knows? One week may turn into years of prayer.

Prayer Cards

Another tool I've found helpful is using prayer cards. I've divided up various prayer requests and needs for each day of the week, following a simple pattern:

- a family member
- a missionary we support
- a ministry we're involved in
- a leader (both in the church and in government)

Our family uses these at morning devotions to help us remember to pray for missionaries, governing officials, pastors, teachers, jobs, ministry endeavors, and one another. We always add in specific and urgent needs such as illness or difficult circumstances, but these prayer cards help us remember to pray faithfully for people (over months and years) even when we may not know their specific needs for that day.

Praying Out Loud

I know it can be awkward to pray alone and pray out loud, but I've found it helpful. Some days I'm too weary or burdened to write, so actually voicing my prayers helps me stay focused in a similar way to writing. I know it may seem strange at first, but I do think it's a helpful way to stay engaged (and awake!) during prayer.

I also do this sometimes when I'm at my computer and a text or email arrives from a friend with difficult news. I simply stop right then and immediately pray out loud for my friend. It helps me take my concerns before the throne of mercy, begging God to work in ways to bring healing, hope, strength, and courage.

Another way we can pray out loud is on the phone or in a conversation with a friend. It's good to pray in our closets, but it's also good to pray with others. I've found that simply asking, "Can I pray for you right now?" is one thing I can do when there is so much else that I can't do. Praying with others can encourage us in the midst of an unwanted struggle.

Pray God's Word

A few years ago, I began the practice of beginning my prayers with the Lord's Prayer. It's not merely a rote exercise but a turning over of my desires. Too often I'm apt to pray, "My will be done," rather than, "Thy will be done." Praying the Lord's Prayer helps me to remember what is important: *May your name be glorified, O God. May your will be done. May your kingdom come.* Thomas à Kempis prayed it beautifully this way:

> Lord, you know what is best. May your will decide what shall be done. Give what you will, how much you will, and when you will. Do what you know is best for me, do what pleases you and brings your name most honour. Put me where you will, and deal with me in all things as you please. I am in your hand—turn me backwards and forwards, turn me upside down. Here I am, your servant, ready for anything, for I have no desire to live for myself, but only to live perfectly and worthily for you.[14]

Beginning my prayers this way helps me to shift my focus off of myself and onto God. It's not that God doesn't want to hear my concerns or anxieties; I know he does. But as I set my heart on what is most important and needed, it changes how I approach prayer. I can't always know what is best, but I know God knows. I can pray for his name to be glorified freely, boldly, eagerly, confidently—with all that is within me.

Praying God's word strengthens and emboldens our prayers. It allows us to pray with a certain confidence that we are asking for a good and right thing. God's word also teaches us how to pray. I've learned to pray from reading the prayers of Daniel, Paul, Hannah, and Jesus. These prayers can guide us as we seek God in prayer.

Whatever we do, may we begin with prayer. Let us hear and obey the words from Jude:

> But you, beloved, building yourselves up in your most holy faith and praying in the Holy Spirit, keep yourselves in the love of God, waiting for the mercy of our Lord Jesus Christ that leads to eternal life. (Jude 20–21)

Before You Meet: Practical Tools to Help You Grow

Take ten minutes and create prayer cards—notecards—to help you pray for each day of the week. You can use the categories I shared or create categories of your own:

- a family member
- a missionary
- a ministry
- a leader (both in the church and in government)

Put these cards in your Bible and use them to help you pray.

While You Meet: Questions for Discussion

1. How would you describe your prayer life? Is praying comfortable for you or is it something you struggle to do?

2. How does knowing you pray to a God who welcomes you with delight encourage you in prayer? Is this difficult for you to believe?

3. What keeps you from prayer? Which of the prayer struggles ("I'm too busy," "It's more important to do something," "I'm easily distracted," or "It's not working") resonates most with you?

4. What disciplines or tools have helped your prayer life? Which of the ideas for growing your prayer life seem like something you'd like to try?

5. What are your top three prayer requests today? Close your time together praying together for each other.

Until You Meet Again: Growing in Godliness
Based on your discussion, consider one area in which you'd like to make a change before you meet next time. It could be to start doing something that will help you grow spiritually or to stop doing something that is preventing your growth. Write it in the space below and discuss it the next time you meet.

7

Family and Friendship

Loving Your Nearest Neighbors

Bearing with one another means we don't expect perfection from our friends in how they relate to us, how they comfort us when we're hurting, how they speak to us, or how they prioritize our friendship. We think the best of our friends and cut them some slack when they don't respond to us perfectly in every situation.

—Christine Hoover

I blame Monopoly. While advertisements proclaim it's a game of family fun, it's pretty clear to me that Monopoly was created to secretly tear families apart. Don't believe me? I'll be glad to give you an example.

It was a quiet afternoon in Charlotte when our family decided it was time for some good old-fashioned family fun. We put away all our electronic devices and pulled out a pile of board games.

Everyone agreed on Monopoly, and we sat down, expecting to make those family memories that everyone remembers with fondness.

We made a memory, all right.

Midway through the game, everyone was mad at someone. While I can't remember all the details, I can (of course!) remember the situation that happened when I landed on my husband's property. I hoped he wouldn't notice, so I quietly and quickly handed him the dice, thinking to myself: *If he rolls, I won't have to pay!*

My daughter—the one that I birthed after thirty-six hours of hard labor—noticed where I was and told my husband just as he was getting ready to roll, "Look where Mom landed, Dad!" My eyes widened with astonishment, hurt, and serious frustration as I cried out, "How could you do that to me?"

I mean, think of all I have done for her for her entire life—diapers, baths, and bedtime prayers. I even made her own baby food. Yet she still chose to betray me. Then my husband defended her cause (I always knew he secretly liked her better than me). All of a sudden, the game erupted into an all-out war. Tears fell, doors slammed, and the game was left abandoned.

So can you see why I blame Monopoly? It's clearly the problem. Right? While I wish it were so, I'm pretty aware that Monopoly was simply a window into the state of my own heart. Even while playing a game (with the people I love most in all the world!), selfish ambition, anger, and envy flared up in my heart. Often it's the people we're closest to that are the most difficult to faithfully love. Our attitudes toward them reveal the reality of what's going on in our hearts. Proximity prevents us from pretending.

When Jesus was asked the question, "What's the greatest commandment?" He replied:

The most important is, "Hear, O Israel: The Lord our God, the Lord is one. And you shall love the Lord your God with all your heart and with all your soul and with all your mind and with all your strength." The second is this: "You shall love your neighbor as yourself." There is no other commandment greater than these. (Mark 12:29)

Simply put, we're to love God and our neighbor. Our nearest neighbors may live next door, or they might live in our very home. Perhaps they sit in the cubicle beside us at work. They see what we do, and they hear what we say. We live life on life with them. Such proximity means that, many days, their will and our will come into conflict.

We'll spend this chapter considering, How do I love my neighbor as myself? Whether we're spending time with parents, best friend, roommate, spouse, or a minivan full of children, we all have relationships that stretch us beyond our capacity to love in our own strength. We'll need the fullness of Christ's love to overflow from us so that we can serve others with joy and kindness rather than bitterness and frustration.

Wisdom for Life

Most of us are painfully aware of the effects of relational brokenness all around us.[15] Too often, love succumbs to anger, faithfulness to betrayal, praise to gossip, and fellowship to loneliness. However, our relationships were meant to be characterized by intimacy and joy. When God created the world, he satisfied the "not good" of Adam's aloneness by creating Eve. Upon completion of creation God saw everything that he had made, and "behold, it was very good" (Gen. 1:31). Adam's need for relationship reflected that he was created in the image of God, who exists as a perfect trinity: Father, Son, and Holy Spirit. We may think we can go it alone, but each of us has an innate need for relationship.

However, since sin entered the picture, every relationship—even the best of relationships—is marred by the painful consequences of Adam's sin. Our relationships with friends, coworkers, parents, children, and spouse suffer from the effects of self-centeredness and pride. The wars we see among nations are just a reflection of the brokenness we have in our homes.

Thankfully, the gospel gives us hope. Rooted in Christ, we're freed to love others with humility and compassion, considering the needs of others before our own. Because our hearts are being renewed, we can put off the old ways of behavior: sexual immorality, envy, anger, slander, lying, and obscene talk and walk in newness of life (Col. 3:5–7).

While those in our families of origin may have related to one another in harmful ways, as part of the family of God, we're a new people with a new way of relating to one another. We may wrestle with old patterns of behavior, but we're no longer enslaved to them. How do we live as the family of God? Colossians 3 directs us in a few specific ways. Paul exhorts:

> Put on then, as God's chosen ones, holy and beloved, compassionate hearts, kindness, humility, meekness, and patience, bearing with one another and, if one has a complaint against another, forgiving each other; as the Lord has forgiven you, so you also must forgive. (Col. 3:12–13)

Be Kind and Compassionate

Our relationships with one another are to be marked by kindness and compassion. When those around us are hurting and suffering, we seek to help. Rather than enviously looking over the fence to see what others have and we don't, as God's people we look over the fence to see how we might care for others.

Compassion notices others. When the crowds had been following Jesus for three days, it would have been easy for Jesus to tell his disciples how worn out he was from teaching and healing people. Instead, he noticed the people and told his disciples, "I have compassion on the crowd because they have been with me now three days and have nothing to eat. And I am unwilling to send them away hungry, lest they faint on the way" (Matt. 15:32).

His inward compassion led him to display outward kindness as he fed the crowds.

Take some time to consider who in your life needs your compassion. How can you extend kindness to them? It might be your three-year-old who is struggling to potty train or your thirteen-year-old whose emotions explode at random intervals. Perhaps it's your roommate who leaves her dishes in the sink or your coworker whom everyone at the office finds annoying. Maybe it's your aunt who calls every day just to check in because she's lonely. Think of one person this week—how can you clothe yourself with compassion and reach out in kindness?

Be Humble and Meek

Humility counts others as more significant than ourselves because we recognize that all the good we have, we've received (Phil. 2:3). We're powerless apart from Christ. In our own strength, we're unable to save ourselves. We can't change ourselves. We're unable to even muster up the tiniest grain of faith—it's a gift. Realizing how much we've been given allows us to rejoice at the good of our neighbor, because their good brings us joy.

This inward humility allows us to walk in meekness before God and others. We put away the deeds of darkness and "receive with meekness the implanted word" (James 1:21). We don't force our own way but live faithfully in light of God's commands. Meekness causes us to be courageously unyielding in our obedience to God while faithfully yielding our preferences for others. It's a formidable strength that bends to wash dirty feet and serves God with gladness.

It's difficult to live in humility and meekness. We want our own will to be done and struggle to prefer the needs of others. Consider someone today that you struggle to view with humility. Perhaps they annoy you, frustrate you, or make the same mistakes over and over. How could you serve them with meekness? How could you put aside your preferences and seek the good of your neighbor today?

Bear with One Another Patiently

Relationships require patience. One friend may continually show up late. Another may say something that unintentionally hurts your feelings. Your husband may have left his towel on the bathroom floor—again. Your children may whine and complain when you tell them no. Your Bible study group leader may have forgotten your name. Your roommate may have come in late and woke you up in the middle of the night.

As God's people we're called to bear with one another in love. We'll need to be gracious and have grace extended to us. Every one of us will unintentionally harm those we love, and we'll be hurt by the careless deeds of others. No person will perfectly love us all the time.

Our impatience often shows up in irritability, anger, arguing, gossip, or frustration. Usually it's the fruit of a prideful heart and judgmental attitude. Patience isn't something we can muster up on our own—it's the fruit of the Spirit alive in our hearts. We'll need God's patience with us as we learn to be patient with one another! Daily recognizing God's forbearance toward us allows us to patiently forbear with others.

Forgive One Another

As the people of God, we walk in forgiveness with one another because we've been so greatly forgiven. We extend to others the mercy we've received. Forgiving people is never an acceptance of their sin. We're not brushing it aside and saying it doesn't matter. Forgiveness means we entrust the wrong committed against us into the hands of God. It doesn't mean that we don't apply the rules of government to criminal wrongdoing; it just means the ultimate judge of sin is God.

God's forgiveness never means acceptance of our sin. He never said, "Oh, that didn't really matter. Don't worry about it!" The cross exposes just how deeply God cares about our sin. God will repay every sinful deed: either by the blood of Jesus (for the believer) or by the blood of the wrongdoer (for the unbeliever). Forgiveness leaves payment in the hands of God: "Beloved, never avenge yourselves, but leave it to the wrath of God, for it is written, 'Vengeance is mine, I will repay, says the Lord'" (Rom. 12:19).

As we live in relationship with others, God clearly commands, "As the Lord has forgiven you, so you also must forgive" (Col. 3:13). It's not a forgiveness for that one time you messed up, but a seventy-seven-times-you-messed-up type of forgiveness (Matt 18:22). We are tempted to keep records of wrongs and replay the failures of others in our mind. Unforgiveness allows sin to fester, breeding anger and discontentment in our heart. Entrust God with past hurts and live in the freedom of forgiveness.

Specific Applications for Relationships

Colossians 3 begins by explaining that because we are part of the family of God, we live differently. As we set our minds on heavenly realities, our earthly lives are changed. We put to death the deeds of darkness and put on compassionate hearts, kindness, humility, meekness, and patience. Our relationship with Christ shapes our relationship with others. Paul then tells us specifically how these principles will work out in the home and in our work. He instructs:

> Let the word of Christ dwell in you richly, teaching and admonishing one another in all wisdom, singing psalms and hymns and spiritual songs, with thankfulness in your hearts to God. And whatever you do, in word or deed, do everything in the name of the Lord Jesus, giving thanks to God the Father through him. Wives, submit to your husbands, as is fitting in the Lord. Husbands, love your wives, and do not be harsh with them. Children, obey your parents in everything, for

this pleases the Lord. Fathers, do not provoke your children, lest they become discouraged. Bondservants, obey in everything those who are your earthly masters, not by way of eye-service, as people-pleasers, but with sincerity of heart, fearing the Lord. (Col. 3:16–22)

There's so much to say about this passage that we can't fully cover in this chapter. However, it's essential to recognize the importance of reading these verses in light of the entire context of the book of Colossians. When these verses are read outside of their context, they can be used to harm, intimidate, control, or coerce—especially when it comes to submission. In the appendix, I've included an article I wrote for The Gospel Coalition that offers a few principles to consider on the topic of submission. Submission applies to every believer in some way, so I encourage you to read it and discuss these principles more fully with your mentor.

Essentially, this passage explains the effects of faith in our homes and jobs. As the word dwells in us richly, our homes look different from other homes. Wives submit willingly, with respect, and husbands love sacrificially, without harshness. Children obey their parents, and fathers patiently instruct their children. We work for others with sincerity and integrity, seeking to please the Lord.

Paul's words to the Colossians may seem outdated or unrealistic, and without the power of the gospel it's a pie-in-the-sky view of family and work. We can't live like this on our own. However, because we are rooted in Christ, everything changes. The Spirit enables transformation in all our relationships, including our most intimate ones. As we walk by faith, new patterns emerge within our home and work. We can work with sincerity and love sacrificially.

Walking in Unbelief

If you're like me, you've probably had the experience of going home as an adult and finding that you quickly revert to your teenage self. I may think I've grown up out of certain behaviors, but then I find myself overly sensitive, selfish, impatient, irritable, unkind, or angry. On a really bad day I might be all of those things rolled up into one.

It's not really just my teenage self that's showing up; it's a battle in my heart between the flesh and the Spirit. While it may be convenient to blame unloving behavior on outward frustrations or circumstances, James tells us, "Each person is tempted when he is lured and enticed by his own desire. Then desire when it has conceived gives birth to sin" (James 1:14–15). Unchecked, these inward desires yield outward harm.

Envy

When Paul wrote to the Corinthians he explained that love doesn't envy. Envy is desire run amok. Rather than hope for our neighbor's good, we hope to possess the good of our neighbor. The quiet war within our heart prevents us from rejoicing with those who rejoice and mourning with those who mourn. We falsely view their good as one more way God has failed to be good to us. Whatever is difficult for them, we see as a minor problem because they have the one thing we desire.

Consider what you are longing for today that someone else has. It may be financial security, marriage, success in your career, children, a home, living in a particular city, or time off for a vacation. How does envy affect your relationships with those who have what you desire? In what way does it keep you from loving them well? Envy doesn't simply stay within our hearts. It always works outwardly into behavior that harms our neighbor.

Irritability

When we're frustrated with our lives or with others, irritability often springs up like a weed in our garden. It may result in harsh words toward our children or gossip about a coworker's annoying habits. We may snap angrily at our husband or say something unkind to our neighbor. Irritability is like a bad cold. It spreads easily and makes everyone miserable. That's why Paul told us that "love is patient and kind. . . . It is not irritable or resentful" (1 Cor. 13:4–5).

It's easy to consider irritability as not a big deal and put it under the heading of "I was just having a bad day." However, the right response is the simple one we often shy away from. When we have allowed our bad day to negatively impact others, the right response is to repent and ask forgiveness, acknowledging that our irritability is unloving and unkind. Confessing our sin, rather than sweeping it under the rug, is how we live out the gospel in the midst of relational mistakes.

Arguing

James warned, "You covet and cannot obtain, so you fight and quarrel" (James 4:2). Selfish desires overflow into arguing and fighting with the people we love. I experienced this painful reality in the early years of marriage when my husband and I moved overseas for his PhD program. I fully believed God was calling him to this program, but I wanted to be back in the States with my friends, working the job I loved. Instead I found myself in a tiny foreign flat with no friends—lonely and seemingly purposeless.

Every inconvenience (and there are many inconveniences when you move overseas) fueled my discontentment, which was then directed at my husband. We argued and fought many times in those first months about a variety of items, but the undercurrent became, "It's your fault this is hard for me." I placed the blame of my discontentment on him rather than diagnosing it as a problem in my own heart.

Consider the most recent argument you had with a friend, parent, coworker, or spouse. How did a clash of desires spark disagreement? It may be easiest to diagnosis the other person's desire problem, but take some time to consider your own. How is not getting what you want in some area leading to arguments with someone you love? It's difficult to look inward, but it's part of learning to walk in love with others.

Walking by Faith: Good News for Grace-Filled Living

We may see our relational failures and wonder, How do I change? I know how hard I've worked to hold my tongue, only to see unkind words bubble up like hot volcanic flow, leaving a path of destruction in their wake. I resonate with Paul's frustration: "For I do not do the good I want, but the evil I do not want is what I keep on doing" (Rom. 7:19).

Perhaps you've experienced the same. You commit to not getting into that political discussion with your uncle during Thanksgiving dinner, but you're barely through your mashed potatoes when you find yourself in the heat of the battle. You want to rejoice with your friend who just got a new, amazing job opportunity, but your own desire for success means you start avoiding her just so you don't have to congratulate her. You want to honor your elderly parents by visiting them regularly but find yourself irritated by their discussion of medicines and doctors' visits.

Is there really hope for change? Can we be kind and compassionate, humble and meek, patient and forgiving? Can we honor our parents, submit to our husband, and love our children well? Thankfully, by God's power we can. Peter promises:

> His divine power has granted to us all things that pertain to life and godliness, through the knowledge of him who called us to his own glory and excellence, by which he has granted to us his precious and very great promises, so that through them you may become partakers of the divine nature, having escaped from the corruption that is in the world because of sinful desire. (2 Pet. 1:3–4)

In Christ we have a new power that helps us grow in godliness. However, it doesn't descend upon us the moment we come to faith. Peter's promise turns to exhortation:

> For this very reason, make every effort to supplement your
> faith with virtue, and virtue with knowledge, and knowledge
> with self-control, and self-control with steadfastness, and
> steadfastness with godliness, and godliness with brotherly af-
> fection, and brotherly affection with love. For if these quali-
> ties are yours and are increasing, they keep you from being
> ineffective or unfruitful in the knowledge of our Lord Jesus
> Christ. (2 Pet. 1:5–8)

Peter directs us to grace-fueled exertion: *make every effort!* The
Christian life is not passive acceptance of sin but an active pursuit
of holiness. It's by grace we believe, and it's by grace that we grow.
However, God uses the means of our effort and striving to grow
us in godliness (Heb. 12:14).

What does this look like in practice? We take hold of the means
God has given us for change. We read his word, we pray, and we
participate in the life of the church. Not only do we read the word;
we obey it. When we sin, we turn back to God in repentance and
confession. Day after day, week after week, year after year, we
press on toward the prize of knowing Christ. Slowly, God changes
us. We may not see immediate change, but over time the effects of
abiding in Jesus bear fruit.

When I was arguing in that Edinburgh flat with my husband,
I thought he was the problem. However, the Lord patiently and
kindly showed me my own problems. At the time, I was reading
through the Bible in a year and one morning turned to this passage: "Be not like a horse or a mule, without understanding, which
must be curbed with bit and bridle, or it will not stay near you"
(Ps. 32:9).

The Spirit convicted my heart: You're the mule, Melissa. Yes,
you've come to Scotland, but you've come fighting like a mule,
resisting along the way. Your problem isn't with your husband;
your problem is with God's will for your life.

Painfully and tenderly the Lord rooted out my sin. Writing
today, some twenty years later, my eyes still fill with tears of

thankfulness at the goodness of his mercy and patience with me. He changed my perspective and worked repentance in my heart. The arguments with my husband didn't stop overnight, but I had a new perspective on why they were happening. Slowly the Lord turned my gaze off of the life I wished I had and turned it back to Jesus, helping me to embrace his plan for my life. God faithfully meets us in our waywardness and puts us on the path of life.

Relationships can be difficult, but they are meant to be a blessing. We need one another. We share in one another's joys, mourn our sorrows, and offer comfort in times of trial. Relationships also expose how much we need Jesus. Ask the Lord for help, wisdom, and guidance as you seek to love your family, friends, and nearest neighbors.

Before You Meet: Practical Tools to Help You Grow

The article I wrote for The Gospel Coalition, "When Callings Clash," is located in appendix 2. As believers, each of us is called to submit in some area. Read this article and consider when submission is problematic as well as how to approach and persuade our God-given authorities. If you're struggling with the topic of submission, make sure to discuss it when you meet together.

While You Meet: Questions for Discussion

1. Which are some of the most significant relationships in your life right now?

2. Read Colossians 3:1–17 together. As you think through your relationships, what is one specific negative trait to "put away" and one positive trait to "put on"?

3. Is there a person with whom you struggle to be patient? What is difficult about that relationship in particular?

4. Are you struggling to forgive someone in your life, or someone whose wrongs you're keeping a record of? What is keeping you from forgiving?

5. In what relationships are you struggling with envy, irritability, or arguing? How is that affecting your relationships?

6. Take some time to pray for each other and the significant relationships in your lives. May God grow your love for those you love.

Until You Meet Again: Growing in Godliness

Based on your discussion, consider one area in which you'd like to make a change before you meet next time. It could be to start doing something that will help you grow spiritually or to stop doing something that is preventing your growth. Write it in the space below and discuss it the next time you meet.

8

Temptations

In the World but Not of It

Satan wants to alienate you from God and claim you for eternity. But Jesus has prayed for you, asking his Father to protect you from the evil one, and you are not at Satan's mercy. . . . Satan may win a battle or two in your life, but he will never win the war against your soul. Jesus has prayed for you, and you are protected.

—*Nancy Guthrie*

I watched the opening scene of the movie *Saving Private Ryan* with tears in my eyes. It vividly displayed the D-Day landing at the beaches of Normandy during World War II. Both of my grandfathers fought in the war, and this scene was a window into the horrors they suffered on the battlefield. Young men ran in terror from boats to the beaches as bullets whizzed by, piercing some, while others continued to press forward. It was painful to watch and difficult to comprehend.

In the midst of such a battle, imagine the surprise we'd all feel if one of the young men stopped on the beach, set out a towel, took off his shirt, and began to put on sunscreen. When a fellow soldier would pause to ask, "What on earth are you doing?" he would reply, "Well, I'm at the beach. I'm going to spend some time enjoying the sun and waves."

Surely the other soldier would look at him with astonishment and reply, "Yes, we're at the beach, but don't you realize there's a war going on? If you just sit here and ignore the battle, you're going to get killed!"

It's difficult to imagine such a scene isn't it? Who would be in the middle of battle and settle in for a day at the beach? Sadly, I think it's the reality for so many of us (myself included) as we go about our lives from day to day. We forget that in the midst of the physical world around us, there's a spiritual battle raging. We think the Christian life is like a nice day at the beach, but it's described as a race (Heb. 12:1–3), childbirth (Rom. 8:22–23), and a battle (Eph. 6:11–23). None of those are easy, and all of them involve pain.

When we forget that the Christian life is a battle, all of life can feel like a surprise attack. Our mistaken understanding of the Christian life as easy and trouble-free can make us question God's goodness when bullets are flying or we're wounded and struggling to take a step forward. We're not prepared for the fight, so we're defenseless against the enemy.

When we understand that we're part of a cosmic war, it changes our perspective—we're battle ready, expecting the attack. It doesn't make the battle any less fierce, but it's much less of a surprise. One of the most important ways to prepare for battle is to understand our enemy and the methods he employs. We'll spend this chapter examining our enemies, considering our unbelief, and training our minds so that we're battle ready to fight temptation.

Wisdom for Life

The Bible warns us that we have three primary enemies that war against our soul: the world, the flesh, and the devil. Each of these adversaries tempts us to sin by walking in opposition to God's word. Every Christian faces temptation. It's not a sin to be tempted—Jesus was tempted by Satan himself. It's when we yield to temptation that we find ourselves caught in the misery of sin. It's helpful to examine each of these enemies so that we learn to recognize their tactics.

The World

When the world was created, it was good. It was made for our enjoyment so that we might glorify God in all we do. However, because of the effects of the fall, the world and its systems press upon us, enticing us toward sin and self-glory rather than godly enjoyment. James warned that friendship with the world is enmity with God (James 4:4), and Jesus taught his disciples that they would be hated by the world. The apostle John explained what is meant by *the world*:

> Do not love the world or the things in the world. If anyone loves the world, the love of the Father is not in him. For all that is in the world—the desires of the flesh and the desires of the eyes and pride of life—is not from the Father but is from the world. And the world is passing away along with its desires, but whoever does the will of God abides forever. (1 John 2:15–17)

The world in this sense isn't about individuals (we're called to love our enemies) but the way the world tempts us with the desires of the flesh, the desire of the eyes, and the pride of life. What our eyes see entices us toward earthly mindedness.

When I look at the world around me, it's easy to desire all that it has to offer. It's tempting to spend all my efforts building my earthly kingdom with a perfectly decorated home, successful career, healthy and delicious meals, and somehow keeping my appearance on trend (and I'm finding it takes an increasing amount of time and energy to even stay above the "she completely let herself go" category).

None of these pursuits are necessarily wrong in and of themselves, but if I spend my life, my efforts, and my days pursuing what the world has to offer, I'll ultimately end up wasting my life. The world can't satisfy, because it's never enough to make us full—it's like trying to fill our tummies by eating the wind. As Puritan minister Thomas Brooks wisely noted, "A man may have enough of the world to sink him—but he can never have enough to satisfy him."[16]

The apostle John reminds us, "The world is passing away." What we can now see will one day be no more. But there's a kingdom we can't see now that will exist for all eternity. It's the kingdom we're called to pursue: "Seek first the kingdom of God and his righteousness, and all these things will be added to you" (Matt. 6:33).

It's hard to seek that which we can't see. It can feel like we're fighting blind. We have to put on our spiritual glasses as we look to Jesus, "the founder and perfecter of our faith, who for the joy that was set before him endured the cross, despising the shame, and is seated at the right hand of the throne of God" (Heb. 12:2). He's the warrior hero who has gone before us and overcome the world. He's our example, our path to follow. We look to him, we fight in his power, and by his grace we overcome the world. We live in the world, but we are citizens of a different land, a heavenly kingdom. If you feel a little lost some days, that's a good sign. You're still searching for home.

The Flesh

The battle we're facing isn't just from the outside, as the world tries to conform us and shape us into its mold. Our flesh battles within us, fighting against the Spirit. Paul explained this inner battle in his letter to the Galatians:

> I say, walk by the Spirit, and you will not gratify the desires of the flesh. For the desires of the flesh are against the Spirit, and the desires of the Spirit are against the flesh, for these are opposed to each other, to keep you from doing the things you want to do. But if you are led by the Spirit, you are not under the law. Now the works of the flesh are evident: sexual immorality, impurity, sensuality, idolatry, sorcery, enmity, strife, jealousy, fits of anger, rivalries, dissensions, divisions, envy, drunkenness, orgies, and things like these. *I warn you, as I warned you before, that those who do such things will not inherit the kingdom of God.* But the fruit of the Spirit is love, joy, peace, patience, kindness, goodness, faithfulness, gentleness, self-control; against such things there is no law. And those who belong to Christ Jesus have crucified the flesh with its passions and desires. (Gal. 5:16–24)

Paul gives a sober warning that if we live by the flesh, we will not inherit the kingdom of God. Now you may look at that list of the works of the flesh with concern because:

- You've been struggling with envy against your friend who just got engaged.
- You slept with your boyfriend, and you know it's wrong.
- You were in a fit of anger at your husband this morning.
- You had that third glass of wine last night and said some things you regret.
- You keep going back to that porn website and can't seem to turn away.

Let me say, just like Paul, that sin is serious. It's walking in unbelief. It's the wide gate that leads to destruction. God's patience with our sin should never be misconstrued as an acceptance of our sin. He doesn't overlook it or ignore it or just pretend that it isn't there. He hates it and empowers us to fight against it. He gives us the Spirit, living inside us to do battle.

If you are caught in sin, I want you to hear two things clearly. First, you are in grave danger; run the other way as fast as you can. The cliff of sin is no precipice on which to play. Don't go near the edge. Don't try to justify your actions. Don't convince yourself it doesn't matter. Repent and return to Jesus. He loves you, he accepts you, and he forgives you. Forsake your sin today and turn to Jesus.

Second, don't despair. Every Christian will battle the old self until we're given new bodies. The war within is evidence of the Spirit's work. We're being conformed into the image of Jesus, but it's a process. Daily we will need to confess, repent, and believe. As Brooks explained, "There's a great difference between a sheep that by weakness falls into the mire and a swine which delights to wallow in it."[17] All of us will fall into sin, but we hate the dirt and keep returning to Jesus to make us clean.

The Devil

We may not talk much of demons and angels in our day and age, but there's a very real spiritual battle happening all around us. Paul explained, "We do not wrestle against flesh and blood, but against the rulers, against the authorities, against the cosmic powers over this present darkness, against the spiritual forces of evil in the heavenly places" (Eph. 6:12).

The devil leads his demonic army as both a tempter and accuser of believers. He wants to make us stumble, and his ultimate goal is our destruction. His plan is to steal, kill, and destroy (John 10:10). Peter warned, "Be sober-minded; be watchful. Your adversary the devil prowls around like a roaring lion, seeking someone to devour" (1 Pet. 5:8).

Satan is relentless in his pursuit. Brooks gives us this insight:

Satan will come on with new temptations when old ones are too weak; in a calm prepare for a storm. The tempter is restless, impudent, and subtle; he will suit his temptations to your constitutions and inclinations. Satan loves to sail with the wind. . . . When you have overcome one temptation you must be ready to enter the [battle] with another.[18]

Satan studies us, looking for our weak spots. He tempts you differently than he tempts me. That's why sometimes it's difficult to understand one another's struggles. One woman may fight against greed in her heart, while another one battles against lust. Just like a fisherman uses different lures for different types of fish, Satan uses different bait to hook his prey.

While Satan's particular temptations for each of us are unique, his aim is usually the same. He wants us to doubt God's goodness and God's word. He knows that doubt leads to distrust and that distrust is the foundation of our disobedience. When we think God is failing to be good to us and that his word isn't certain, we'll more readily be led astray.

Satan will pursue us, but he has no true power over us. James gives us this insight: "Submit yourselves therefore to God. Resist the devil, and he will flee from you" (James 4:7). As we submit ourselves to God's word, Satan will flee. He can't force us to sin, and his lies only have power when we listen to them. We can be on the lookout for his attack, but we do not have to fear his advance.

Wandering in Unbelief

The Allies' success at Normandy on D-Day didn't just happen because they fought bravely during the attack. For months beforehand, German spies that had been turned by British intelligence fed false information back to the Nazis about invasion plans and troop movements. This faulty information prevented the Germans from consolidating their troops in one place. Instead, their army was spread out over 1,500 miles of coastal defenses. Because the Nazis listened and believed the lies, they were left unprepared for the attack.[19] Spreading disinformation is a powerful part of war strategy.

Satan uses similar tactics to confuse and disorient God's people. The "father of lies" (John 8:44) subverts the truth of God's word to lead us astray, particularly when it comes to our understanding of sin. He takes truth and twists it just enough so that we'll believe his falsehoods. Following are a few of the lies he whispers to keep us wandering in unbelief.

Lie: "God Is Merciful, So Your Sin Doesn't Matter"

This lie has a partial truth, so it makes it all the more convincing. God is merciful—more than we can even fully comprehend. However, his mercy doesn't drive us further into sin; it drives us into a life of repentance (Rom. 2:4) and sacrificial service. Paul exhorts, "I appeal to you therefore, brothers, by the mercies of God, to present your bodies as a living sacrifice, holy and acceptable to God, which is your spiritual worship" (Rom. 12:1). Do you see what he's saying here? God's mercy doesn't lead us to keep on sinning. (May it never be so!) A true understanding of God's mercy propels us to boldly lay down our lives. We don't live for the flesh any longer. Instead, we sacrifice our flesh and live by the Spirit.

Lie: "It's Just a Little Sin"

We tend to keep a hierarchical system of sins in our minds, don't we? Adultery, well, that's bad. Stealing, murder, and lying—those are bad too. But a lustful thought here or there, a little gossip with friends over dinner, or a few too many glasses of wine—well, those aren't big deals (we tell ourselves). They're just little sins. They aren't harming anyone else, right?

Again, Satan masquerades his lies with partial truths. It is true that some sins are more heinous than others.[20] It is worse to murder than to punch. However, both actions are sinful. Both are enough to eternally separate us from God. And here's the thing about sin: it never stays small. We can't manage it or tame it. Like Frodo's ring, it begins to rule us. Yielding to temptation allows a foothold for more sin. Just as one tiny cancer cell multiplies and can kill the strongest, healthiest man, so sin acts as a cancer on our soul. Fight every sin—even the ones that seem small—at first attack.

Lie: "Other Christians Think It's Okay"

We live in a world that increasingly lives by one law: *Be true to yourself.* This false ideology creates confusion when we look around our world. Many claim Christ, but their lives seem untouched by the effects of the Spirit's work. They live in ways that directly contradict God's word and invite us to follow in their version of Christianity. However, we cannot look to those who merely profess faith to be our guides in Christian living. We look to the Bible. It is our guide, our standard, our example.

Ultimately—it doesn't matter what other people think is right or wrong. It matters what God thinks is right or wrong. He made us. He knows us. His ways will always be proven right. Don't follow the crowd into sin because it looks like an easier path. As Jesus taught, "The gate is wide and the way is easy that leads to destruction, and those who enter by it are many. For the gate is narrow and the way is hard that leads to life, and those who find it are few" (Matt. 7:13–14).

Your path of obedience may be the road no one else is taking. It may be difficult. It's made even harder still by others telling you there's no need to be on it. Don't listen to the Sirens that sing, leading you to the cliffs of death. The narrow gate leads to Jesus, and he leads you to fullness of life.

Lie: "My Temptation Is Harder"

One of the lies that I'm most prone to listen to is rooted in my pride. I can say to myself, *This temptation is too hard to bear. Anyone else dealing with this would sin too!* I think one of most humbling verses (and hopeful ones) in all of Scripture is 1 Corinthians 10:13:

No temptation has overtaken you that is not *common to man*. God is faithful, and he will not let you be tempted beyond your ability, but with the temptation he will also provide the way of escape, that you may be able to endure it.

It's rather shocking to learn that our temptations are common. Let me tell you how much I want to explain to you that my temptation is not common. I convince myself: *If your kids had acted like my kids, you would have yelled too. If you had a boss like mine, you'd gossip about him as well. If you had a friend like mine (the one who gets everything she wants), you'd envy her too.* My temptation is simply harder than your temptation, so of course I'm going to fall into the trap.

This verse boldly sets us straight. Nope, your temptation isn't harder than someone else's. It's common. Other people have had this same struggle. And no matter your particular struggle, there's another needed nugget of truth that offers freedom: God will not let you be tempted beyond your ability.

Do you hear that good news? Your Creator knows you better than you know yourself. He knows exactly what you can bear, and he's going to help you escape it and endure it. You may not feel that you can fight one day longer, but God knows exactly what he's doing. You have a power beyond your own ability to help you in the fight. He will provide all you need. And the first thing he helps you to do is get dressed for battle.

Walking by Faith: Good News for Grace-Filled Living

Last week my cell phone died. I felt somewhat powerless. What if my kids called from school and couldn't reach me? What if I missed a work email? What if I got stuck waiting in line somewhere and didn't have Instagram to relieve my boredom? (Let's be honest: I was probably more worried about the last one than the first two.) My phone was in perfect working order except for one thing—I had forgotten to plug it in the night before. Everything that my phone has power to do was dismantled by my forgetfulness.

In our fight against sin, we sometimes forget the good news. We have one who has gone before us. Jesus resisted the world and defeated the devil, and through his flesh he made a way so that we can draw near in full assurance of faith, with our hearts sprinkled clean from an evil conscience (Heb. 10:19–22). The blood of Jesus paid the penalty for our sin and freed us from its power over us.

Yet some days we feel powerless—like a phone that didn't get charged the night before. We're battle worn and weary, unsure how to access the power we've been given. Thankfully, Paul tells us how to fight, and his first piece of advice is to get dressed: "Put on the whole armor of God, that you may be able to stand against the schemes of the devil" (Eph. 6:11).

Many days I forget to put on my armor. I have an entire outfit waiting for me, but I go out to face the world spiritually naked, and I'm left powerless against the foe. I have access to the power, but if I forget to use it, then I'm left vulnerable to attack. How do we prepare? What do we put on?

As our "Before you meet" activity this week, we'll walk through the armor of God and discuss how to apply it specifically to a sin you're currently struggling to fight. We'll take this passage line by line and use it as a helpful tool to resist the enemy. We have the power; we just need to learn how to use it. We've studied our enemy, now let's get dressed for battle.

Before You Meet: Practical Tools to Help You Grow

Think of one specific sin you're battling right now. Let's go through this passage and apply it to the struggle you're facing.

Put on the belt of truth. "Stand therefore, having fastened on the belt of truth . . ." (Eph. 6:14). The belt holds the rest of the armor in place. What truth do you need to fasten in your mind today to help you in the battle? Write it out now and remind yourself of this truth throughout the day.

Put on the breastplate of righteousness. ". . . and having put on the breastplate of righteousness . . ." (Eph. 6:14). The breastplate protects the heart and other vital organs. Christ's righteousness is what protects our soul. We rest on his perfection, not our own. How can understanding that you are already *declared* righteous help you as you strive to *live* righteously today?

Put on shoes for your feet. ". . . and, as shoes for your feet, having put on the readiness given by the gospel of peace" (Eph. 6:15). It's hard to fight a battle without the right footwear. How does remembering the good news of the gospel of peace give you readiness to fight today?

Put on the shield of faith. "In all circumstances take up the shield of faith, with which you can extinguish all the flaming darts of the evil one" (Eph. 6:16). The enemy will send his flaming arrows of lies your way. He will declare that God isn't good or that God's word isn't best. Reflect on God's goodness to you. What can you thank him for today to remind yourself of his faithfulness?

Put on the helmet of salvation. ". . . and take the helmet of salvation . . ." (Eph. 6:17). Your mind is one of the most important parts of the battle, and it needs protection. Satan wants you to doubt your salvation. He'll tell you you're not good enough, worthy enough, or strong enough to fight. How does remembering that salvation is by grace alone through faith alone (and not by your works) protect your mind from the lies of the enemy?

Put on the sword. ". . . and the sword of the Spirit, which is the word of God . . ." (Eph. 6:17). While all the other parts of the armor are defensive, we have one weapon of offense: God's word. What particular verse can help you in battle today? Look it up now and write it out, meditating on it throughout the day.

Put on prayer and perseverance. ". . . praying at all times in the Spirit, with all prayer and supplication. To that end, keep alert with all perseverance, making supplication for all the saints" (Eph. 6:18). We need God's armor, and we need his help, so we pray in the Spirit. As eighteenth-century author Anne Dutton wrote, "Let us watch and pray that we enter not into temptation, that we yield not to the suggestions of Satan or any of his instruments to draw us away from God. But let us stand as holy warriors, with our armor on, resisting the devil and opposing the powers of darkness to the utmost."[21] Take time now to plead with God to help you in the fight. Pray also for each other, that God will help both of you persevere in the fight against temptation today.

While You Meet: Questions for Discussion

1. In what area are you struggling most with temptation?

2. Is there any repetitive sin you need to confess and repent of? I encourage you not to wait until your next meeting; confess it today. Sin keeps us in fear and bondage; seek the freedom that comes through confession and repentance.

3. How do you see temptation at work in your life through the world, the flesh, or the devil?

4. Which of the four lies outlined in the chapter are you most likely to struggle with during temptation? Or is there another one that keeps you stuck in sin?

5. How does God's word combat the lies of Satan? What verse is helping you currently as you fight sin?

Until You Meet Again: Growing in Godliness

Based on your discussion, consider one area in which you'd like to make a change before you meet next time. It could be to start doing something that will help you grow spiritually or to stop doing something that is preventing your growth. Write it in the space below and discuss it the next time you meet.

9

Joy in the Journey

Cultivating Contentment in All Seasons

The tension you feel as you try to simultaneously hope in heaven while living wholeheartedly in this life isn't necessarily an indicator of sinful discontentment. It may simply be evidence that you are a citizen of heaven living on earth.

—*Betsy Howard*

Picture with me for a moment a woman standing at the edge of the ocean with a cup in her hand. She's desperately thirsty. She thinks to herself, *The water looks so refreshing. If I can just have a drink, surely it will satisfy my thirst.* She reaches down and fills her glass and brings the salt water to her lips.

At this point, we'd want to cry out and tell her, "Don't drink the water! It may look refreshing, but it will only make you thirstier. And if you keep drinking it, you will die."

We would say this to her not because the ocean is bad. In fact, the ocean is quite good. The ocean is beautiful to behold, wonderful for play, and beneficial for all sorts of marine life (some of which I pretend do not exist every time I go for a swim). While the ocean is full of many good things, it was never intended to satisfy our thirst. If we use it in a way it wasn't created to be enjoyed, it will actually harm us.

We're often like this woman. We know that we are thirsty, but we keep going to the wrong places to try to find refreshment. We think that if we can get all our circumstances sorted out, then our life would be easier, more carefree, more content. Today you probably have some longing or difficulty in your life that, if removed, you believe you'd finally be content, satisfied from your thirst.

However, contentment doesn't come from a perfect set of circumstances (just ask Eve), and most of the places we go searching for refreshment only make us thirstier. It's not that our longings are necessarily bad or sinful; most of them are good things. However, we tend to expect too much from them. Relationships, success, financial security, beautiful homes, and a life of comfort are simply unable to satisfy our thirst. They may temporarily bring us happiness, but we will always find ourselves wanting more. Sometimes I feel like I'm the most unsatisfiable creature in the world.

However, our problem isn't that we are thirsty. Our thirst is natural—we're longing for something better for a good reason. This world is broken, and it's full of hardship, trials, and lives that don't go as we planned. Our problem is where we keep trying to go to find a drink.

One of my favorite invitations is found in Isaiah 55:1–3, a passage we looked at earlier. It's an invitation for thirsty people:

> Come, everyone who thirsts,
>> come to the waters;

and he who has no money,
  come, buy and eat!
Come, buy wine and milk
  without money and without price.
Why do you spend your money for that which is not bread,
  and your labor for that which does not satisfy?
Listen diligently to me, and eat what is good,
  and delight yourselves in rich food.
Incline your ear, and come to me;
  hear, that your soul may live. (Isa. 55:1–3)

It's wonderful to be invited to something, isn't it? It's all the more wonderful when someone tells you, "Just come. Don't bring a thing. All we want is for you to come and enjoy." What a gift it is to be invited to a rich banquet without money and without cost. You may find yourself asking, "Where's the party?" Thankfully, Isaiah tells us:

Seek the LORD while he may be found;
  call upon him while he is near;
let the wicked forsake his way,
  and the unrighteous man his thoughts;
let him return to the LORD, that he may have compassion
    on him,
  and to our God, for he will abundantly pardon.
    (Isa. 55:6–7)

Isaiah points us to the true fountain of living water, the spring from which we were created to drink: God. Only God can satisfy us in a way that makes us truly content. All other places we seek refreshment will ultimately leave us unsatisfied and wanting more. God, and God alone, is the source of our contentment. Only when we drink of him will we find life, and find it to the full.

You may think to yourself, "Well, I've come to God, I've believed in Jesus, and I'm still thirsty." Just like we eat in the morning and find ourselves hungry by noon, our walk with

God is a continual coming to him. Jesus described himself as the bread of life and giver of living water (John 6:48; 7:37). These are images of the daily physical sustenance we need in order to live. We need daily spiritual refreshment from Jesus so that our souls can truly live, delighting in the richest of fare. We'll spend this chapter seeking to understand true contentment and our misunderstanding of contentment, as well as how our growing understanding of God's character is the source of our contentment.

Wisdom for Life

One of my favorite images of contentment in Scripture is from Psalm 1 and Jeremiah 17. Both passages paint the picture of a tree planted by a stream. When the heat and drought come, this tree has nothing to fear because it has the refreshment of the stream. No matter what happens, it bears fruit, and its leaves do not wither. Psalm 1 tells us that this is the picture of a person who delights in God's word, meditating on it day and night. Jeremiah 17 tells us this is a person who trusts in the Lord.

If we want to be contented people who are always bearing fruit, our trust will be in the Lord and our delight in his word. The definition I like to use for biblical contentment is this:

> Biblical contentment is an inward trust in God's sovereignty and goodness that produces the fruit of joy and peace and thanksgiving in the life of a believer, regardless of outward circumstances.

Our contentment isn't rooted in our circumstances but in the unchanging nature of our God. As we know him more, we trust him more. Contentment is a settled spirit, a quiet confidence that God is always at work for good. Paul was an example of this type of contentment. He wrote to his beloved Philippians from inside a Roman jail. His outer circumstances were bleak, but he was filled with inner joy and peace. He told them his secret:

Not that I am speaking of being in need, for I have learned in whatever situation I am to be content. I know how to be brought low, and I know how to abound. In any and every circumstance, I have learned the secret of facing plenty and hunger, abundance and need. I can do all things through him who strengthens me. (Phil. 4:11–13)

We'll consider three hopeful truths from this passage as we consider contentment.

Contentment Is Available in Christ

You may hear this from Paul and think to yourself, "Well, of course he can face these trials and still be content; he's a super apostle! I mean, he wrote most of the New Testament. I'm just an ordinary person. I could never be content like that." However, Paul's contentment wasn't rooted in his own identity; it was rooted in Christ's.

Paul wasn't just a naturally contented, laid-back sort of guy. His contentment came from a source outside of himself. Just like the tree planted by the stream continually bears fruit, Paul was planted in Christ, and this—not his natural disposition or even his apostleship—fueled his contentment.

Here's the good news: you and I have the exact same resource available to us. Christ is in us, empowering us to endure all circumstances and still bear fruit. He gives us strength when our strength is gone.

Contentment Is Independent of Circumstances

Paul told the Philippians that his contentment was independent of both plenty and want. We naturally tend to think of its being difficult to be content when we're in need. However, both plenty and want can make us discontented.

You may be facing circumstances today that make life seem unbearable. You may feel that you can't endure one more day.

I think Paul would understand with compassion and kindness. He knew suffering. He was beaten, whipped, shipwrecked, and hungry, and faced danger from people and circumstances at every turn (2 Cor. 11:24–28). Only Christ can fuel our contentment in difficult circumstances. He promises strength for today. Don't look to tomorrow. He is able to provide all you need.

While most of us can quickly understand why it's difficult to be content when life is hard, it's also helpful to consider the difficulty of contentment in times of plenty. As many of us know, there are struggles with getting what we hoped for:

- We may have gotten married after years of waiting but find the blessing of marriage and family its own struggle. In the fullness of family life, we can struggle to be content.

- We may have longed for financial security and finally feel secure but now face the burden of responsibility to manage well what we've been given and worked so hard to gain. In the fullness of wealth, we can struggle to be content.

- We may have longed for success and finally achieved it but now face the reality of people wanting our advice and influence. In the fullness of success there are added burdens that can make contentment difficult.

Just as sunshine is warm and brings life but can also cause a sunburn and drought, having plenty is no solution for discontentment. In our fullness we often forget our need of Christ and fail to seek him. As Thomas à Kempis aptly states, "You cannot find complete satisfaction in any temporal gift, because you were not created to find your delight in them. Even if you possessed all the good things God has created, you could not feel happy and glad; all your gladness and happiness rest in the God who created those things."[22]

Neither plenty nor want defines Paul's contentment. He was content because he had access to the strength of Christ. To use our earlier imagery: Christ was the stream from which Paul drew his strength. It's from this stream we must continually drink if we ever want to be full.

Contentment Is Learned

When my son was born, he didn't come out quietly into the world. He came out screaming. He didn't have to be taught that the world isn't right; he seemed to know it intuitively. However, it took him six weeks to learn how to smile. By nature, we are discontented creatures. I find it so encouraging that Paul tells us that he *learned* contentment. It didn't come to him as soon as he became a Christian. As he walked through various circumstances in life, he learned to depend on Christ.

When was the last time you learned something new? As we get older, we tend to stick with what we know and forget that learning is hard work and usually involves a lot of failure. If you've ever listened to someone learn a new instrument, you know what I mean. You can't expect to play all the notes perfectly the first time you pick up an instrument. It takes years of practice—years of off-note, rather screechy performances—before someone can play with ease and beauty.

You may think you are the slowest student ever in the school of contentment (although, I'm pretty sure I have you beat). That's okay—learning takes time. I used to tell my math students that when they reached that point of frustration—the moment when they most wanted to throw their pencil in the air and quit altogether—that was the very point at which they were learning something new. But it's hard. Learning stretches us beyond what we think we're capable of doing.

Your circumstances today are your schoolroom for contentment. You may not like the course load you've been given, but there are reasons for the lesson. God has a purpose for whatever you're facing today. As J. I. Packer said:

Perhaps He means to strengthen us in patience, good humour, compassion, humility or meekness. . . . Perhaps He has new lessons in self-denial and self-distrust to teach us. Perhaps he wishes to break us of complacency or undetected forms of pride and conceit. Perhaps His purpose is simply to draw us closer to Himself. . . . Or perhaps God is preparing us for forms of service of which at present we have no inkling.[23]

Whether you are in need or in plenty today, trust in God. Delight in his word; meditate on it day and night. He will strengthen and supply all you need. Your work is to abide in him.

Wandering in Unbelief

One of our greatest struggles with contentment is that we often have an incorrect picture of what it means to be content. It's helpful to understand what something *is not* in order to have a more correct understanding of what *it is*. Paul learned contentment, but we can gain a better picture of what that really looked like from what he shared about his life with the churches to whom he wrote. From Paul's letters, below are four things contentment is not.

1. Contentment Is Not a Carefree Existence

Contentment isn't having it all together and finding a life of perfect balance. Nor is it an idyllic moment spent swinging on a hammock, sipping lemonade, and reading a book on a cool fall afternoon, while all the world around you falls apart. Paul's description of his time in Asia probably wouldn't make the Facebook feed:

> For we do not want you to be ignorant, brothers, of the affliction we experienced in Asia. For we were so utterly burdened beyond our strength that we despaired of life itself. (2 Cor. 1:8)

Burdened, afflicted, despairing—these descriptions are not in opposition to a contented soul. In this world we won't be free of hardship. Contentment trusts God while walking through the hard. Joy and sorrow can walk side by side and not be in opposition to each other.

2. Contentment Is Not the Absence of Relational Conflicts and Anguish of Heart

Paul had his share of relational disagreements, even departing from Barnabas over a dispute regarding Mark (Acts 15:39). In the midst of deep affection, ministry included relational anguish:

> I wrote to you out of much affliction and anguish of heart and with many tears, not to cause you pain but to let you know the abundant love that I have for you. (2 Cor. 2:4)

Loving others means our hearts will be for them. Contentment is not an indifferent disposition toward others. Instead, we should expect that the depth of our love for one another will involve tears—we weep when others weep and feel compassion in their pain. Contentment is not in opposition to longing for the day when heartache will be over and tears will be no more.

3. Contentment Is Not a Life without Longing and Groaning in Our Distress

When we mistakenly view contentment as an endlessly positive Pollyanna attitude, we miss entering more deeply into relationship with Jesus. Jesus was troubled in soul on the eve of his crucifixion and in agony prayed multiple times to the Father for rescue (Luke 22:44). Paul described his own experience with similar distress: "In this tent we groan, longing to put on our heavenly dwelling" (2 Cor. 5:2).

Contentment does not mean that we are free from desires, longings, or heart-wrenching circumstances. If you are hurting or someone you love needs healing, cry out to God in prayer. Contentment isn't apathy or a sort of "grin and bear it" mentality. We can seek solutions and help in our trials. We can tell others we are suffering. Crying out to God for relief is not in opposition to contentment.

4. Contentment Is Not Freedom from Fear and Anxiety

Paul explained the state of his circumstances and inner turmoil in stark detail:

> Even when we came into Macedonia, our bodies had no rest, but we were afflicted at every turn—fighting without and fear within. (2 Cor. 7:5)

Paul faced outward danger and inward fear. He bore daily pressure and anxiety for all the churches under his care (2 Cor. 11:28). He did not hide his struggles, both physical and emotional. Yet he took his fears and anxieties to the Lord and experienced peace in the midst of them. As he instructed the Philippians:

> Do not be anxious about anything, but in everything by prayer and supplication with thanksgiving let your requests be made known to God. And the peace of God, which surpasses all understanding, will guard your hearts and your minds in Christ Jesus. (Phil. 4:6–7)

Paul learned the secret of contentment not by freeing himself from earthly struggles or burdens but by experiencing the power of Christ's presence in both his times of plenty and times of want. He embraced Christ's goodness in the midst of life's hardness. All of Paul's life testified: *Christ is enough. It is well with my soul.*

Walking by Faith: Good News for Grace-Filled Living

A few years ago, I moved into a new home. The day of the closing ended up being the very day I had to leave for a church retreat in another city. I signed the papers with my husband and then headed out of town. To my dismay, I left my new kitchen in a complete mess.

Thankfully, our new home was directly behind the home of one of my good friends. We've walked life together for years, and she knows me better than I know myself sometimes. While I was out of town she came over and unpacked my kitchen for me. She did it just like I would have done—in fact, better in some ways. It is good to be known, isn't it? I felt so loved by my friend, not just because of her service to me but because she knew what I needed and how to care for me well.

While a good friend might know us well enough to organize our kitchen, God knows everything about us. He's the master potter; we are the clay. He knows just what we are composed of, our frame, what we can bear, and his purposes for our lives. He arranges all our circumstances with wisdom and insight beyond our ability to understand. Only a God who knows everything can do this well. The foundation of our contentment is not a new set of circumstances but a growing understanding of God's character. The more we know who he is, the more we learn to trust him.

Every summer we spend days enjoying my parents' boat on the coast of North Carolina. We always put two anchors in the water when we come to land so that we'll be protected from the currents that would cause the boat to drift or run aground. There are two anchors of God's character that hold me fast when life is hard and I don't understand what he's doing: God's sovereignty and his goodness. These two anchors will keep us secure in the most troubling of seas.

His Sovereignty

By God's *sovereignty*, I mean all the truths about God that make God different from us. God knows all things. He can do all things. He's everywhere. He's Creator. God is God. He's the king over all the universe and reigns supreme. Nothing happens to you or me outside of his plan.

Now, there are times when I see what God is doing in my life and I think he got the wrong address. I question his judgments and ways of working in my life. I forget that I am finite and limited in my understanding. I think I know better. Many days I'm like a two-year-old child throwing a tantrum because I want to play in the street but have no understanding of the danger. However, God knows all things and can do all things. He knows my story from beginning to end. He knows what is best, while I can only understand what looks good to me for today.

Understanding God's sovereignty sturdies our faith when trials come. Whatever we are enduring is not random; it's carefully planned. Nothing can happen to us outside of God's plan for our lives. From the traffic we face on the way to work, to the painful heartache we endure, God is at work. He never wastes an ounce of our pain—our trials, tears, and temptations are sifted through his loving hands.

His Goodness

God's sovereignty might be a terrifying thing if it were not also linked to his goodness. Not only is God in control of all the events of our lives; he works them all for good (Rom. 8:28). His good might not always look like what we want it to look like. I might be quite content to have my life look just like my neighbor Jane's life. However, God will not let me settle for a lesser life. He wants my best life—he wants me to look like Jesus.

When we believe that God is working for our good, we endure hardship in new ways. If he chooses to withhold something we have longed for, we trust it must be because he has some purpose that we cannot currently understand. Belief in God changes everything. We begin to realize that the bedrock of our contentment isn't the goodness of our day but the goodness of our God.

In contrast, our lack of contentment is rooted in unbelief. We feel disappointed with God, and our discontentment festers into distrust. Distrust breeds disobedience. Rather than walk with God in our struggle, we turn from God and go our own way. (This pattern of disappointment → discontentment → distrust → disobedience pretty much sums up the Israelites in the Old Testament.)

How do we fight against this pattern of unbelief? Whenever I'm tempted to doubt God's goodness, I go back to the cross. There's no greater display of God's goodness and sovereignty than the cross of Christ. Speaking at Pentecost Peter declared, "This man was handed over to you by God's set purpose and foreknowledge; and you, with the help of wicked men, put him to death by nailing him to the cross" (Acts 2:23).

The cross of Christ was not a random act of violence that God worked for good. Paul asserts it was a providentially planned event, ordained by God's set purpose that he worked for good. The most evil event that has ever occurred in human history happened in accordance with God's set purpose. In the mystery of his providence, he worked the actions of wicked men for good so that he might rescue us from death. God used death to defeat death.

Why did he do it? He did it for our good, so that we could have eternity with him. Whenever I'm tempted to believe that I'm missing out on something in this life or that God doesn't really care about me, the cross reminds me of what I've been given. If God didn't spare his own Son for my sake, can't I trust him with what he withholds? As Paul questioned, "He who did not spare his own Son but gave him up for us all, how will he not also with him graciously give us all things?" (Rom. 8:32).

Present contentment is rooted in a past reality (the cross of Christ) and a future hope (an eternity with Christ). To have contentment today, we look back to the cross, remembering the love that purchased our freedom, and we look forward to a day when all things will be right. Future hope yields present joy. However, we have to train our minds to remember and rejoice. It takes time.

Our contentment displays Christ's power at work in our hearts. It's a living testimony to his grace. Shine the good news with gladness: you've been rescued. You've been redeemed. You're on your way home. The hope we display is an irrepressible witness to the watching world.

Before You Meet: Practical Tools to Help You Grow

E. B. Pusey, an Anglican pastor, gave the following guidelines for growing in contentment. Read through them and consider how they might help you grow in contentment.

1. Allow thyself to complain of nothing, not even the weather.
2. Never picture thyself to thyself under any circumstance in which thou are not.
3. Never compare thine own lot with that of another.
4. Never allow thyself to dwell on the wish that this or that had been, or were, otherwise than it was, or is. God Almighty loves thee better and more wisely than thou doest thyself.
5. Never dwell on the morrow. Remember that it is God's not thine. The heaviest part of sorrow often is to look forward to it. "The Lord will provide."[24]

While You Meet: Questions for Discussion

1. In what ways do you struggle with contentment?

2. How do you tend to express discontentment?

3. How does Paul's life display that contentment isn't about having perfect circumstances?

4. How does understanding God's sovereignty and goodness grow contentment?

5. How does the cross assure you of God's love for you?

6. Spend some time praying that the Lord would help you learn contentment in the areas that are currently a struggle.

Until You Meet Again: Growing in Godliness

Based on your discussion, consider one area in which you'd like to make a change before you meet next time. It could be to start doing something that will help you grow spiritually or to stop doing something that is preventing your growth. Write it in the space below and discuss it the next time you meet.

10

Service

Spending Your Life on Others

Our hope is eternal and not dependent on immediate gratification or successes. Keep standing, keep serving, keep working diligently unto the Lord. The One we serve stands victorious over sin and death and is faithful to produce fruit in His good time and in accordance with His purpose. When we know that to be true, no labor done unto the Lord is ever in vain.

—*Ruth Chou Simmons*

I walked out of the doctor's office in tears of frustration. I'd been going from doctor to doctor about various random ailments—an unrelenting cough, uncomfortable stomach issues, unsightly facial rash—and now this doctor wanted to send me to another doctor for more tests. I was weary of doctor visits that didn't seem to be helping in the midst of an already jam-packed schedule and overly long to-do list.

That evening, in an effort to clear my mind, I decided to go for a run. I was about two songs into my playlist when I turned into a new neighborhood that was being constructed next door to mine. As I came down the hill and off the curb onto the road, I stumbled slightly. At that moment, I felt sharp pain in my ankle and heard a crack reverberate through my body. When I tried to put weight on my ankle, I nearly crumbled to the ground. I knew it meant another trip to another doctor.

X-rays proved what I feared: my ankle was broken. I spent the next three weeks on crutches, and then the next nine weeks after that clomping around in a large boot. One tiny broken bone made simple tasks difficult. On crutches, I couldn't carry my cup of tea from the kitchen counter to my desk (my rolling office chair became my temporary wheel chair). Activities like taking a shower, getting in the car, or going upstairs all became exceedingly difficult. My entire body suffered aches and pains from compensating for what my ankle could no longer do.

In a tangible way, my broken ankle helped me understand the importance of every part of my body. To be in good health, I need everything working well, down to the smallest cell. When one part is missing or unable to work correctly, it puts a greater strain on every other part. It also inhibits my ability to help and care for others.

Paul used the analogy of the body to explain how we work together in the church (1 Cor. 12). We're created and gifted to be a part of something bigger than ourselves. We're to use our gifts to serve others and be a blessing to the world around us. If one person's service is missing, we all suffer—both in the church and in the world.

We'll spend this chapter considering the part each of us is called to play as we serve others. You may feel like the smallest, most insignificant member of Christ's body, but your life matters.

Christ set his love upon you, came to earth to rescue you, and died so that you might have life. You're part of the greatest story ever told. In Christ, our seemingly insignificant lives burst forth with meaning and purpose.

Wisdom for Life

Jesus told his disciples, "By this all people will know that you are my disciples, if you have love for one another" (John 13:35). This type of love was displayed in the early church:

> They were selling their possessions and belongings and distributing the proceeds to all, as any had need. And day by day, attending the temple together and breaking bread in their homes, they received their food with glad and generous hearts, praising God and having favor with all the people. And the Lord added to their number day by day those who were being saved. (Acts 2:45–47)

The early disciples gave generously and gladly to one another, and people around them noticed. The love and service we offer to one another within the church is one of the greatest witnesses to the watching world. Considering the needs of others before our own isn't the way the world usually works. The world exhorts us to use our time, talents, and treasure to build up ourselves and seek personal greatness through fame, power, and the accumulation of wealth.

In contrast, as believers, we steward our time, talents, and treasure in service to others. We follow the kingdom values of Jesus, who lovingly displayed the pathway to true greatness as he washed dirty feet and suffered the shame of the cross. His example illuminates his teaching: "The greatest among you shall be your servant" (Matt. 23:11).

The Bible shows us a variety of ways we can lovingly serve others as we steward the time, talents, and treasure the Lord has given to us.

Our Time

Time is one of those things we can quickly fritter away. It's easy to spend thirty minutes shuffling through social media, a couple of hours shopping, or an entire day binge-watching the new Netflix show that everyone's talking about. We think of time off work as *our* time—we even call it "free time." We can do with it whatever we want, right? However, time is actually one of the most limited resources we have. We may gain new talents, and we may increase our treasure, but every day we have less time. It's not a recyclable or renewable resource. Our days are limited. The psalmist prayed, "O Lord, make me know my end and what is the measure of my days; let me know how fleeting I am!" (Ps. 39:4); and, "Teach us to number our days that we may get a heart of wisdom" (Ps. 90:12).

Many in the world recognize the brevity of life and make the decision to live each day to satisfy their own desires. Since life is short, their advice is to enjoy that piece of cake, leave that annoying spouse, or travel the world. Others try to extend their days through healthy living. Some try to prevent any signs of aging by surgeries that nip and tuck. However, no matter what we do, the clock is ticking.

As Christians, we have a different understanding of time. Paul warned the Ephesians, "Look carefully then how you walk, not as unwise but as wise, making the best use of the time, because the days are evil" (Eph. 5:15). You can almost hear him pleading: *Don't waste your life!* We've been given time here to use for kingdom purposes. We've got one life to live, and our understanding of God's eternal plan changes how we use the time we've been given.

In his first letter to the Corinthian church, Paul reminds them of the glorious reality of Christ's resurrection and the hope it gives to all who belong to Christ. Just as Christ was raised from the dead, we will be raised from the dead. Just as he was given a new body, we will be given new bodies. Our bodies may taste physical death, but they will be raised to eternal life.

Resurrection truth changes everything. Our time on earth may be limited, but our days of living are eternal. We don't need plastic surgery to keep our bodies pristine, because we'll be given new bodies. We don't have to travel to every country or experience everything now, because we have an eternity to savor and enjoy God's creation. How do we live in light of this reality? Paul tells us, "Therefore, my beloved brothers, be steadfast, immovable, always abounding in the work of the Lord, knowing that in the Lord your labor is not in vain" (1 Cor. 15:58).

Rather than use your time to build your own kingdom that can never last, use your time to abound in the work of the Lord. It's not a wasted life. It's the only life that makes sense. Death is coming, but it's been swallowed up in victory. Take the time you've been given and make it count—not in earthly treasure, where moth and rust destroy, but in heavenly treasure. Your time here can be used to store up treasure there, that you'll get to enjoy forever. There's no better investment.

Our Talents

Paul writes to the church at Corinth, explaining that each person is gifted to serve the church. We don't all serve in the same way, but we all serve in some way. We're also all empowered in the same way: "Now there are varieties of gifts, but the same Spirit; and there are varieties of service, but the same Lord; and there are varieties of activities, but it is the same God who empowers them all in everyone" (1 Cor. 12:4–6).

We're to use the gift we've been given to serve others for the common good. We each bring something to the table and together everyone benefits. It's helpful to think through how we're best able to serve, not to limit our service but so that we steward our service well. If a foot started trying to act like a hand, it would only be able to do so much. Can you imagine writing a letter with a foot? It might be able to happen, but it wouldn't be the best use of your foot!

141

Peter tells us we're to be good stewards of God's varied grace as we serve one another (1 Pet. 4:10). That means we don't just say yes to every service opportunity. We thoughtfully consider how to best serve others, just like we thoughtfully consider how to spend our money. This doesn't keep us from doing the tasks that need doing (we can all pitch in when chairs need to be put away or serve in the nursery), but we think through the best use of our gifts for the sake of others. If you're good with numbers, you might serve on the budget committee. If your strength is teaching, you may lead a Bible study. If you're gifted in hospitality, you may open up your apartment to pray for others.

Every person is different when it comes to service. You may be a "Yes, of course I will" type of person who jumps into service and overcommits to too many good things (I'm right there with you). Or you may be the type who defaults with a no and needs to be encouraged to say yes. If you're not sure where to serve, ask someone in the church what's needed and plug in there. Your church needs your service.

Our Treasure

According to Crown Financial Ministries, the Bible has over 2,350 verses about money.[25] These verses explain both the positive and negative realities about wealth as well as guide us as we steward our financial resources. Money in and of itself isn't bad. In fact, it can be a reward for a life of faithfulness. Proverbs instructs: "The crown of the wise is their wealth" (14:24) and "The diligent man will get precious wealth" (12:27).

At the same time, money can be a stumbling block for those who put their trust in it. We're warned that the love of money will never satisfy (Eccles. 5:10) and that it's the root of all kinds of evils (1 Tim. 6:10). Jesus taught his disciples, "No servant can serve two masters, for either he will hate the one and love the other, or he will be devoted to the one and despise the other. You cannot serve God and money" (Luke 16:13).

Money is powerful because it can so easily become our security. While US coins declare, "In God We Trust," the reality most of us live is, "In Money We Trust." Money offers tangible benefits— it promises ease, comfort, pleasure, security, power, and prestige. Our hearts can so easily be drawn toward a love of money because we can quickly recognize all that it provides.

Hebrews exhorts us, "Keep your life free from love of money, and be content with what you have, for he has said, 'I will never leave you nor forsake you'" (Heb. 13:5). God's presence in our lives secures contentment in a way that money never can. Financial fortunes may change, but God will never leave us. We have nothing to fear, because our true provider is always present.

One way we actively put our trust in God and keep our lives free from the love of money is by giving it away. The Israelites were instructed to give ten percent of their earnings back to God as an offering. Proverbs instructs, "Honor the LORD with your wealth and with the firstfruits of all your produce" (Prov. 3:9). Paul commended the generous offering of the Philippians as they supported his missionary efforts (Phil. 4:14–18) and instructed the Corinthians to set aside money to give on the first day of every week (1 Cor. 16:1–2). As we follow their examples and give money back to God, we remember and recognize him as the ultimate provider of all we have.

As we give our money to support the work of the church, the church can then use its resources to bless the world. Together as a body, we can do more together than most of us can do on our own. Church ministries help care for the poor, the hurting, the lost, and the displaced. Through missions we support the work of the church as it travels to unreached people groups. How we use our money impacts so many. Being thoughtful in how we spend allows us to be generous in how we give.

Wandering in Unbelief

It's difficult to steward our time, talents, and treasure well in a world that invites us to self-satisfaction and self-fulfillment.

Perhaps the most countercultural thing we can do is to humbly serve others without thinking of ourselves. However, there are a few lies that keep us from service.

Lie: "In This Season I Don't Have Time"

Whatever season you're in, I'm sure you're busy. Your days overflow with demands from work, friends, family, and errands to do. It's easy to raise the white flag in surrender and tell ourselves we'll just have to wait to serve others at another time. Right now, we're too busy, overwhelmed, and worn out. What we need is a Netflix binge, not more opportunities to serve. We assure ourselves that in the next season we'll have more time to serve others.

However, I've found that there's never a perfect season for serving others. While there are some seasons that particularly stretch us, usually we're pretty good at filling any free parts of our schedule with something we enjoy. We may think next year will have an abundance of time, but it actually may have less time because of unexpected struggles or trials.

Here's the reality: service to others comes at a cost to ourselves. We surrender how we'd like to use our time in order to give it away to others. It's not an easy choice to make. It forces us to lift our eyes off ourselves and onto Jesus, who for the joy set before him endured the cross. He gave his life in service to you and me. We can be radical in how we use our day today because we know eternity awaits.

Lie: "My Service Doesn't Matter"

In my current season I spend a lot of time traveling and teaching the Bible to women. My time on the road means I'm not always able to bring a meal to a hurting friend or volunteer in certain ways. I know it may sound exciting to travel and teach, but sometimes I struggle with the feeling that my work really doesn't matter. Since I can't always see the effects, I question if the hours of preparation are worth it. I wonder if anyone even remembers what

I said after I leave. I can look at some of my other friends who serve in more tangible ways in our community and think to myself, *They are the ones doing the real ministry.*

You may feel the same way about your service. Maybe you deal with chronic pain that prevents you from many forms of service, but you faithfully pray for others daily from your couch. Perhaps you patiently listen to the struggles of others and offer wise counsel. Perhaps you've taught the same children's Sunday school class for thirty years at church and know all the children by name. Your service may seem hidden or insignificant, but God sees your efforts and knows your deeds done in humility. Many small acts of service build a vibrant church, change the surrounding community, and impact the world.

Lie: "God Doesn't Need My Money"

When it comes to giving our money away, it's tempting to think it doesn't really matter. If God owns the cattle on a thousand hills (Ps. 50:10), why does he need our money? Of course God doesn't need our money, but he does use our money as a means by which he accomplishes his purposes.

More than that, money acts as a barometer for our faith. We give because the Spirit is alive in our hearts. As we are increasingly changed into the image of Jesus, we increasingly reflect the generosity of our Savior, and that overflows into monetary giving.

We may think to ourselves, *I'll give more when I have more.* However, it's important to realize that it's difficult for both the rich and the poor to give. While we might assume it's easier for the wealthy to give, it was the rich ruler who left Jesus very sad because he couldn't imagine giving away his wealth (Luke 18:18–20). In contrast, the poor widow was commended by Jesus: "Truly, I tell you, this poor widow has put in more than all of them. For they all contributed out of their abundance, but she out of her poverty put in all she had to live on" (Luke 21:3).

Jesus knows what it costs you to give from what you have. He's not asking you to give because he needs your money. He's asking you to give because it's good for your soul. The faithful act of giving builds faith. It also builds joy, for as anyone who gives generously can tell you, "It is more blessed to give than to receive" (Acts 20:35).

Walking by Faith: Good News for Grace-Filled Living

As we walk by faith, we become people who give to others. We share our time, our talents, and our treasure to care for those in our church and those in the world. Not only do we give, but we do so cheerfully, generously, sacrificially, and lovingly. Our attitude matters as we give. It's the overflow of a heart that delights to share with others out of the abundance we have received.

Generously and Cheerfully

In the midst of severe affliction and poverty, the Macedonian church gave joyfully as God's grace overflowed from their lives. How could they give in such a way in the midst of their own suffering? God was at work in and through them. He supplied so they could give: "You will be enriched in every way to be generous in every way, which through us will produce thanksgiving to God" (2 Cor. 9:11). God gives to us so that we can give to others so that others will give thanksgiving to God.

How we give matters. Paul explained, "Each one must give as he has decided in his heart, not reluctantly or under compulsion, for God loves a cheerful giver" (2 Cor. 9:7). This verse doesn't mean that we wait until we feel cheerful and then give. It means that if we're giving without joy, we need to do a heart check. Giving is an act of worship. If we're cheerless in our service, it says something about our attitude toward God. Ask God to fill you with a deeper understanding of all that is yours in Christ. We don't serve to be seen or receive praise from others but in overflow of praise to God.

Sacrificially and Lovingly

Paul wrote, "I appeal to you therefore, brothers, by the mercies of God, to present your bodies as a living sacrifice, holy and acceptable to God, which is your spiritual worship" (Rom. 12:1). Gospel-centered giving is costly giving. It requires sacrifice.

It's an uncomfortable question to ask ourselves, but it's one that needs asking: *How sacrificial is my giving? What is it costing me today to serve others?*

I tend to want to run from these words of Jesus: "If anyone would come after me, let him deny himself and take up his cross daily and follow me" (Luke 9:23). I long for comfort and ease, and cross bearing sounds difficult and painful. However, in the upside-down way of the gospel, as we lay down our lives, death to self gives birth to life. We may feel like we're being consumed, but we do not lose heart. Even if the outer self is wasting away, our inner self is being renewed day by day (2 Cor. 4:16).

We give sacrificially because we love others. In both Romans 12 and 1 Corinthians 12 Paul uses the analogy of the body to explain how we're all to serve one another. In both instances, he concludes by exhorting them to love one another. First Corinthians 13 (the wonderful passage explaining love) flows out of Paul's teaching on service. He concludes 1 Corinthians 12 by telling them that the most excellent way they can serve is to love (v. 31). If we're in Christ, no matter what particular gifting we may individually have, we're all equipped to love. It's our family resemblance and the common DNA we share.

We've been blessed to be a blessing. In whatever way we serve with our time, talents, or treasure, let us do so with generosity, cheerfulness, sacrifice, and love. As we reflect the love we've been given, our service shines to the watching world.

Before You Meet: Practical Tools to Help You Grow
Option 1: Spiritual Gift Test

You may not have a good sense of your spiritual gifts, but there are helpful online tools that can give you direction. Before you meet with your mentor, take a spiritual gift test such as those offered at the website of Team Ministry or Explore the Bible.[26]

Option 2: Money Management

If you want to focus on stewarding money, I encourage you to visit The Truth Project website and complete the document "God's Pattern for Financial Success."[27]

Option 3: Time Management

If you're concerned about your time, I encourage you to think through how you spent your time last week and ask yourself:

1. What are the two biggest time wasters in my life?
2. What's one creative way I could use my time more wisely? (For instance, if you have a long commute, you might listen to a sermon or a podcast).
3. What do I need to spend less time doing and what do I need to spend more time doing next week?

While You Meet: Questions for Discussion

1. Review the "Growing in Godliness" activity from your last meeting. Have you seen progress in that area?

2. Do you realize your service is important, or do you struggle to think you matter in your church? How has God gifted you to serve others? How are you currently serving in the church and in your community?

3. Which area is the hardest for you to give to others: time, talent, or treasure? Which of the optional activities did you complete? How was that helpful?

4. What are the biggest time wasters in your life?

5. In what ways would you like to be more generous with your money?

6. Would you describe your service as generous, cheerful, sacrificial, and loving? Which of these descriptors do you struggle with the most? In what area—time, treasure, or talents?

Until You Meet Again: Growing in Godliness

Based on your discussion, consider one area in which you'd like to make a change before you meet next time. It could be to start doing something that will help you grow spiritually or to stop doing something that is preventing your growth. Write it in the space below and discuss it the next time you meet.

11

Discernment

Choosing What Is Best

The goal of discernment is not to simply avoid the evil in this life; it is to learn what is good so that we might embrace and enjoy it.

—*Hannah Anderson*

This morning I woke up, fixed a pot of tea, and made a breakfast of Greek yogurt, strawberries, and a little bit of honey. It was a conscious, thoughtful decision. I knew the yogurt would provide protein for my body, the strawberries would give me antioxidants and vitamins, and the honey would give the meal a hint of sweetness to make it more enjoyable.

I also knew that if I waited until I was out and about, busy with my day, I'd be tempted to stop and pick up a mocha at the local coffee store and a doughnut (or two, because one is never enough when you're really hungry). While those are enjoyable treats, if I make the daily choice to listen to my cravings instead of what is truly good for my body, then slowly, over time, my body won't work quite as well. On that very day I'll become sluggish after my mocha-doughnut sugar crash, and over time I'll increasingly gain weight, which will eventually put strain on all the other parts of my body. What I do today matters for how I'll enjoy tomorrow.

Each and every day, we make small decisions that add up to a lifetime of living. The longer we're alive and the more wisdom we gain, the more equipped we are to discern what is best. I know about the sugar crash that follows a couple of doughnuts because I've experienced it—many times. I know about the health benefits of eating well because I've read articles and gained knowledge. A balanced combination of knowledge, understanding, wisdom, and experience overflows into discernment.

Just like it's not sinful to have a doughnut, many of the spiritual decisions we make each day aren't necessarily choices between right and wrong. However, the accumulation of these choices yields powerful results over the long haul. The small choices we make matter: *Do I read* People *magazine or a daily devotional with my morning coffee? Do I scroll through Instagram or memorize Scripture while I'm waiting in line? Do I spend my money here or there? Do I put on the latest Top 40 song or listen to worship music?* It's not the one-time individual choice but a lifetime of making choices that leads us on a trajectory toward spiritual growth or away from it.

We also have big, life-altering choices to make: *What job should I take? Whom should I marry? Where should I live?* For the many daily decisions we have before us—big or small—we need discernment. We'll spend this chapter considering what discernment is and how to get it, ways to discern the voice of false teachers, and the impact discernment has on our lives as we walk by faith.

Wisdom for Life

We live in the age of information. We can access all sorts of statistics with the simple press of a button. Actually, we don't even have to press a button anymore—we can just ask Alexa. We have more data than ever before available to us. However, it's also become increasingly difficult to discern fact from fiction and truth from falsehood. In the midst of much good and helpful information, we live in the era of false news, fake websites, and internet scams that seek to deceive.

In his book *The Discipline of Spiritual Discernment*, author Tim Challies offers a helpful definition: "Discernment is the skill of understanding and applying God's Word with the purpose of separating truth from error and right from wrong."[28]

Both our thinking and our living need discernment because thinking truthfully will help us to live rightly. It's why Paul emphasized the importance of keeping a close watch on our lives and our doctrine (1 Tim. 4:16). Both matter, and each one impacts the other.

For a more simplistic definition, I like to say that *discernment is wisdom making a choice*. Each day we choose what we think about and how we live. Discernment is the application of wisdom to our choices, from whom we marry to what we listen to on the radio.

Proverbs 9 speaks to the reality that there are two voices calling out to each of us every day, inviting us to listen. The first voice vying for our attention is wisdom:

Wisdom has built her house;
    she has hewn her seven pillars.
She has slaughtered her beasts; she has mixed her wine;
    she has also set her table.
She has sent out her young women to call
    from the highest places in the town,
"Whoever is simple, let him turn in here!"
    To him who lacks sense she says,
"Come, eat of my bread
    and drink of the wine I have mixed.

Leave your simple ways, and live,
and walk in the way of insight." (vv. 1–6)

Wisdom cries out for our attention, promising life. But, there's another voice calling:

The woman Folly is loud;
she is seductive and knows nothing.
She sits at the door of her house;
she takes a seat on the highest places of the town,
calling to those who pass by,
who are going straight on their way,
"Whoever is simple, let him turn in here!"
And to him who lacks sense she says,
"Stolen water is sweet,
and bread eaten in secret is pleasant."
But he does not know that the dead are there,
that her guests are in the depths of Sheol. (vv. 13–18)

As we look at these two passages, notice that both Wisdom and Folly cry aloud, inviting us into their homes. They also both invite the same people (compare verses 4 and 16): *the simple and those who lack sense.* Unfortunately, that's us. We're limited, finite, simple creatures. Even the most brilliant among us has inadequate understanding and perspective.

However, wisdom and folly differ in one important way—what they offer. The way of wisdom leads to life, while the path of folly leads to death. That means there's a crucial choice before us. The invitation we accept is of the utmost consequence. How do simple people choose wisdom? How do we discern the voice of truth from the voice of folly?

Thankfully, the passage points us to the solution. In between these two invitations, right in the middle of this proverb, we're told: "The fear of the LORD is the beginning of wisdom, and the knowledge of the Holy One is insight" (Prov. 9:10).

If we want to find life and choose the better portion, we start with God. Our fear of him isn't a craven fear that runs from God but a reverent fear that draws us near to God. We listen to his word as those who recognize that though we are simple, God is not. He is infinite, all-knowing, and full of wisdom, insight, and truth. His ways are firm, and he knows all things, and he created all things. God's word gives us something more than another point of view. It gives us access to God's infinite understanding. Our dependence on God's word makes us wise. Listening to it helps us to know God's voice so we can discern between wisdom and folly as they cry out.

It's important to clarify that discernment doesn't necessarily result from age, experience, travel, reading, or advanced degrees. Some very experienced, educated, and well-read people spend their entire lives making very bad choices. Experience and knowledge can offer us some insight, but they're inconsequential in comparison to the word of God. Age might make us know more than a twenty-year-old, but it's just one tiny drop of insight, whereas God's word has an ocean of understanding from which we can draw.

As we walk with God, learning from him and growing in our understanding of him, we grow in discernment. It's a skill that is gained as it's put into practice. The writer to the Hebrews explained it this way:

> Though by this time you ought to be teachers, you need someone to teach you again the basic principles of the oracles of God. You need milk, not solid food, for everyone who lives on milk is unskilled in the word of righteousness, since he is a child. But solid food is for the mature, for those who have their powers of discernment trained by constant practice to distinguish good from evil. (Heb. 5:12–14)

Not everyone graduates from milk to solid food. Discernment is learned as we apply God's word to all the decisions we make each day—from the books we read to the job we take. It takes constant practice to distinguish good from evil and apply God's word to all parts of our lives.

When I was first learning to cook, I spent a lot of time reading recipes and following them precisely. They helped me gain a general understanding of how to put flavors together. However, the older I get, the less I follow recipes. I can taste a sauce and know it needs some red pepper flakes, oregano, garlic, salt, or pepper. Over time I've learned to discern what's missing and know what's needed.

Discernment in the Christian life works in a similar way. It takes both knowledge and constant practice to learn how to distinguish good from evil. Over time, the eternal wisdom we gain from God's word increases our situational wisdom for everyday decisions. We'll be able to "taste" our circumstances and more quickly discern what is best. We'll also be able to more quickly understand false wisdom when it comes knocking at our door. And if there's one thing we can be sure of, it's this: folly will come knocking, inviting us to its feast of death.

Walking in Unbelief

As we seek to engage with the world around us and make wise decisions, it's important to recognize that there's not just false news in the world; there are false teachers in the church. We have a plethora of publishers and podcasts promoting people as believers whose lives do not reflect the teachings of Jesus. Their misguided words impact both our thinking and our living. To help us discern how to listen carefully, I'll offer three principles about false teachers, as well as four ways to spot them.

Principle 1: False Teachers Look Like Christians

We may think it's always safe to listen to voices inside the church, but Jesus warned us to be on our guard, "Beware of false prophets, who come to you in sheep's clothing but inwardly are ravenous wolves. You will recognize them by their fruits" (Matt. 7:15).

One of the most difficult realities about false teachers is that they look like real Christians. We'll find them enjoyable and likeable. They'll talk the talk of Christianity, and their lives may seem to reflect a vibrant faith, but eventually their fruit will expose them. Remember Judas? He followed Jesus for three years. He was sent out by Jesus to heal the sick, raise the dead, and cast out demons (Matt. 10:5). When Jesus told the disciples that one of them would betray him, none of them knew who it would be (John 12:22). Instead they all pointed to themselves, asking Jesus, "Is it I?" (Mark 14:19).

These men traveled with Judas, ministered with Judas, and lived day in and day out with Judas for three years. Yet none of them knew he was a false follower of Jesus. Surely they were shocked and distressed when they realized his betrayal. It's painful to realize that people you respect and admire might not be who they say they are. However, we all need to be aware of the reality that some who seem close to Jesus are not truly following him. Many may have an outward connection with Jesus but lack an inward affection for Jesus. Eventually, the fruit of their choices will expose them.

Principle 2: False Teachers Have a Following

A second reality about false teachers is that people want what they're teaching. Paul warned Timothy, "The time is coming when people will not endure sound teaching, but having itching ears they will accumulate for themselves teachers to suit their own passions, and will turn away from listening to the truth and wander off into myths" (2 Tim. 4:3–4).

When you see people running after a new teaching, it doesn't mean you should follow just because it's popular. Some teachers will take the Bible and twist it to suit their own ends as well as the desires of their listeners. Christianity is a historic faith, with beliefs that transcend cultures and communities. While we may express old truths in new ways, we're not looking for new truth. We should be concerned when teaching departs from historic biblical doctrine.

Principle 3: False Teachers Are Eventually Revealed

Jesus, Paul, and Peter all warned against false teachers. Their instruction reminds us to be on guard. However, we also need to be discerning as we interact with incorrect teaching. We're not commanded to scroll through Twitter with theological guns blazing, ready to shoot down every false statement uttered. It's important to remember that every *mistaken* teacher isn't a *false* teacher.

In the book of Acts, Luke tells us the story of Apollos, an eloquent man, competent in the Scriptures. However, his teaching wasn't fully correct, because he only knew of the baptism of John. We're told, "He began to speak boldly in the synagogue, but when Priscilla and Aquila heard him, they took him aside and explained to him the way of God more accurately" (Acts 18:26). Apollos's teaching wasn't fully right. However, he wasn't a false teacher; he just needed to grow in his understanding. All of us will make mistakes theologically. Even though I've tried to be faithful to the Scriptures, I've probably made mistakes as I've written this book!

This reality exposes our need for situational wisdom. I wouldn't necessarily dismiss someone's teaching because of one incorrect statement. However, over time, we can begin to recognize certain signs that help us spot the difference between a false teacher and a mistaken teacher.

Sign 1: False teachers are unwilling to respond to correction. One sign of false teachers is their response to correction. Apollos received the correction from Priscilla and Aquila and went on to greatly help the church in Achaia (Acts 18:27). Godly teachers who may have some theological errors are thankful when they receive correction. They are aware of their own need for growth. In contrast, false teachers refuse to be corrected. When confronted with error, they dig in deeper, unwilling to listen to others who think differently from themselves.

Sign 2: False teachers sit above God's word rather than under God's word. False teachers cherry-pick passages to suit their own ends. They take Bible verses out of context to prove their point rather than humbly submit to the whole counsel of God. In a sense, they position themselves above God's word because they are using it to prove their point rather than learning from God's word by humbly allowing it to teach, correct, and rebuke. False teachers use Scripture to win an argument while failing to listen to and learn from it themselves.

Sign 3: False teachers depart from historical Christianity. Christianity has a long history. Over centuries theological truths have been debated and discussed. Theological errors often resurface with slight variations for a new generation. While these errors may gain traction for a season, over time truth wins. When a Bible teacher claims to have a new interpretation that departs from historic Christianity, we should be immediately concerned—especially if the new teaching aligns more with changing cultural norms than biblical truth.

Sign 4: Eventually false teachers' lives will expose the fruit of their belief. Peter warns us: "False prophets also arose among the people, just as there will be false teachers among you, who will secretly bring in destructive heresies, even denying the Master who bought them, bringing upon themselves swift destruction. And many will follow their sensuality, and because of them the way of truth will be blasphemed. And in their greed they will exploit you with false words. Their condemnation from long ago is not idle, and their destruction is not asleep" (2 Pet. 2:1–3).

Peter's words help us understand the fruit that eventually exposes false teachers: pride, sex, and money. In their pride, false teachers deny the teaching of Jesus and blaspheme the way of truth. They tell you of their love for Jesus while teaching in opposition to his word. Second, they follow a path of sensuality. Usually either their teaching on sexuality or their practice of sexuality is in opposition to the Bible. Last, false teachers are lovers of money. Their greed for wealth leads them to exploit their followers.

Unfortunately, false teachers live among us in the church, affecting how we think about and live in the world. Their words cast doubt and confusion on the Bible. Over time their false words and lives are exposed, but we also want to learn ourselves how to quickly distinguish truth from error and right from wrong. We want to be able to "taste" that something is off theologically. Sometimes the biggest influencers in our lives aren't the books we're reading or the teaching we're hearing but the friends we're chatting with over lunch. How do we practically grow in our ability to discern what advice to listen to and what to reject?

Walking by Faith: Good News for Grace-Filled Living

When my friend Angela first graduated from college, she worked as a bank teller. She spent weeks in training before actually working with customers. One thing that surprised me was the training method used to help employees spot counterfeit money. For weeks, the tellers worked only with real money. They were taught all that was true about each different bill—what special marks to look for on each one they received. They were never shown a counterfeit bill in the initial training.

Eventually, the trainers began to sneak in counterfeit bills alongside the real ones. Angela told me that after weeks of looking only at real bills, it was simple to spot the fakes, even the good ones. Her mind was so aware of what to look for, she could easily identify what was false, no matter how creative someone might be.

There was a reason the bank taught them in this manner. There are numerous ways people can make counterfeit money. Thieves are increasingly creative in their work. However, only one type of money is true. The best way to discern what is false is to be so familiar with what is true that you can immediately spot it.

The same is true for us as we seek to recognize false teaching. Satan is crafty in his deception. He's the father of lies and twists Scripture to suit his nefarious purpose—our destruction (John 10:10). The best way we can grow in our discernment is to be students of truth. Where do we find truth? We find it in God's word.

To become discerning, we need God's word in every way we can get it. If you think back about this book, God's word has been the consistent thread for spiritual growth.

- We read, study, and memorize God's word on our own (chapter 3).
- We hear God's word taught and study it with others in the church (chapter 4).
- We share God's word with others as we evangelize (chapter 5).
- We speak God's word as we pour out our hearts to God in prayer (chapter 6).
- We live God's word as we love our friends and family (chapter 7).
- We wield God's word as our sword in fighting temptation (chapter 8).
- We remember God's word as we trust God for contentment (chapter 9).
- We participate in the power of God's word as we serve in the church (chapter 10).

God's word is vital for discernment. Hebrews 2:4 tells us, "The word of God is living and active, sharper than any two-edged sword, piercing to the division of soul and of spirit, of joints and of marrow, and discerning the thoughts and intentions of the heart."

The Bible guides us in the truth and leads us on the path of life. It's how Jesus speaks to us today. God's word protects us by filling our minds with truth so we can more easily spot what is false. It's impossible to have spiritual discernment apart from God's word.

We can also ask God for discernment. Just as Paul prayed for his beloved Philippians, so we can pray for one another:

> It is my prayer that your love may abound more and more, with knowledge and all discernment, so that you may approve what is excellent, and so be pure and blameless for the day of Christ, filled with the fruit of righteousness that comes through Jesus Christ, to the glory and praise of God. (Phil. 1:9–11)

Growing in discernment doesn't promise us an easy, trouble-free life. But it does lead to a fruitful life—one that is lived to the glory and praise of God.

A final way for us to walk with discernment is to pursue and listen to older saints in the church (which is my hope in writing this book!) Older believers have so much to offer. They've seen good desires go unfulfilled, lost loved ones, struggled in their marriages, battled cancer, prayed for prodigal children, and experienced job loss. They've also witnessed God's presence and provision at every step along the way. It may be tempting to listen to the thirty-something online with a lot of flashy advice, but I encourage you to reach out to an older woman in your church. Ask for her guidance, prayers, and wisdom as you seek to discern what is best.

As we conclude this book, you may be wondering, do these small daily choices matter? Yes, they do! I've been walking with the Lord for over thirty years. In many ways, this book is a summation of everything I've built my life on as I've trusted God. These are the truths I most want to share with younger women in my life.

Can I tell you something? I don't regret one moment of walking with God and for making time in his presence my first priority. His ways are true. His path is secure. He's lovelier to me today than when my soul first received the good news. He's the fount of living water, the continual feast we get to enjoy, and the author of all that's good. The simple daily steps of Bible reading, church attendance, evangelism, prayer, loving others, fighting temptation, serving in the church, learning contentment, and growing in discernment lead us on the path of blessing because they lead us to Jesus. It may not look like the most exciting life, but there's no better way to live. Trust him, follow him, and cling to truth:

> Blessed is the man
>> who walks not in the counsel of the wicked,
> nor stands in the way of sinners,
>> nor sits in the seat of scoffers;
> but his delight is in the law of the LORD,
>> and on his law he meditates day and night.
>
> He is like a tree
>> planted by streams of water
> that yields its fruit in its season,
>> and its leaf does not wither.
> In all that he does, he prospers. (Ps. 1:1–3)

Before You Meet: Practical Tools to Help You Grow

For the mentee: go back through the various weeks of this study and consider how time with your mentor has helped you grow in discernment. What specific pieces of advice and words of wisdom have helped you? Write them in the space below and share them with your mentor at the next meeting.

For the mentor: how has this journey with a younger woman been a blessing for you? How have you grown in the process? What words of encouragement can you offer?

While You Meet: Questions for Discussion

1. For what current situations in your life do you need discernment?

2. How have you seen small patterns and decisions have a big impact over time (for good or for bad)?

3. Have you ever been impacted by false teaching? How so?

4. Why is it so important to be a discerning reader?

5. How does what we think affect how we live?

6. To gain discernment, we need God's word, God's people, and prayer. Which of these areas do you need to grow in most?

Until You Meet Again: Growing in Godliness

Take some time to discuss your plans. Will you continue to meet or take a break? What would you like to study next? Think through ideas and then pray for one another. Thank God for the various ways he has allowed you to grow together during this season of mentoring.

Acknowledgments

As I finish this book, I am thankful. The Lord has met me in tender ways along this journey and once again shown me that he is able to do immeasurably more than all I ask or imagine.

The Lord provided encouraging friends to walk alongside me. Tracy Thornton and Angela Queen read as I wrote and offered encouraging feedback and helpful editing advice. I'm thankful for Elizabeth Poplin and Wallace Barnes convincing me to include the final chapter on discernment—it was a needed addition! Behind the scenes are the faithful prayers and words of support of Uptown's Women's Care Team, especially my coworkers Ginni Fischer and Stephanie Kraska; Susan Foster; Trillia Newbell; Anne Rogers; Chris Vaughn; Erica Crumpler; Kate Willis; Lisa Marie Ferguson; Kimberly Curlin; Peggy Chapman; Macon Collins; Ashley Mink; Dottie Bryan; Lisa Cosper; Anne Abner; Teresa Davis; Amy Henderson; Lauren Palmer; Shanna Davis; and Beth Herring. I treasure your friendship and needed every one of your prayers! When I write, it's your stories I remember, your faces I see, and your friendship that spurs me on in the race. Thank you for faithfully walking with God and loving others—it's my joy and delight to partner in the gospel with you.

I have the privilege of working alongside excellent editors and gifted writers at The Gospel Coalition. I owe a special thank you to Collin Hansen for encouraging my writing (and making it better) and for the entire team praying for me in this project. Sarah Zylstra, Betsy Howard, Taylor Turkington, Megan Hill,

Ann Westrate, and Courtney Doctor, it's a gift to work with each of you. Thank you for encouraging me and praying for this project. Also, it's a privilege to be a part of the Reformed Theological Seminary family. They cheer me on (especially our chancellor, Ligon Duncan) and provide excellent resources that helped in the writing of this book.

I am indebted to both Robert Wolgemuth and Austin Wilson for their helpful assistance and advice. They handle all the details of the publishing process so well and give me the freedom to focus on writing. Thank you for all you do.

I've truly enjoyed getting to work with the entire Crossway team on this project. I'm thankful to Dave DeWit for his vision for this book and valuable guidance. In addition to helpful editing advice, Lydia Brownback has provided kind encouragement in the writing process. I'm grateful for this opportunity to partner together.

I'm particularly thankful for the encouragement and mentoring I've received throughout the years. Tracey Moore, Deanne Trollinger, Connice Dyar, Nancy Guthrie, and Jen Wilkin, thank you for investing in me. Your love for God, his people, and his word has impacted me in so many ways. Thank you for taking the time to "call back" to me and encourage me in the race.

My family was incredibly supportive while I was working on this project. My parents, Bob and Anita Bryan, cheer me on in everything I do. My children—Emma, John, and Kate—bring daily joy and laughter into my life. They prayed for me, wrote loving notes, and cheerfully let me spend Saturdays writing.

I couldn't do any of the writing I do without the support of my husband, Mike. He prays for me, helps me find time to write, and patiently answers all the theological and biblical questions I regularly send his way. He's my best friend, faithful encourager, and friendly editor—he makes my writing better in every way. I'm so thankful to walk this journey with him.

And to my readers, thank you. So many of you have written me letters of encouragement after reading my other books. Often the notes came to my inbox just when I was feeling discouraged or didn't particularly feel like writing. Thank you for reminding me why I write.

For all those seeking to grow together, this is my prayer:

I thank my God always when I remember you in my prayers, because I hear of your love and of the faith that you have toward the Lord Jesus and for all the saints, and I pray that the sharing of your faith may become effective for the full knowledge of every good thing that is in us for the sake of Christ. For I have derived much joy and comfort from your love, my brother, because the hearts of the saints have been refreshed through you. (Philem. 4–7)

May the Lord bless you and encourage you!

Appendix 1

Recommended Reading

Chapter 1: We Need One Another

Hunt, Susan. *Spiritual Mothering: The Titus 2 Model for Women Mentoring Women*. Wheaton, IL: Crossway, 1992.

Chapter 2: Setting Expectations and Sharing Your Story

Furman, Gloria, and Kathleen Nielson, eds. *Word-Filled Women's Ministry: Loving and Serving the Church*. Wheaton, IL: Crossway, 2015.

Kruger, Melissa, ed. *Identity Theft: Reclaiming the Truth of our Identity in Christ*. La Grange, KY: The Gospel Coalition, 2018.

Chapter 3: Taste and See: Savoring the Word of God

Arthur, Kay. *Lord, Teach Me to Study the Bible in 28 Days*. Eugene, OR: Harvest, 2008.

Wilkin, Jen. *Women of the Word: How to Study the Bible with Both Our Hearts and Our Minds*. Wheaton, IL: Crossway, 2014.

These authors offer study guides on different books of the Bible or biblical topics that can help you grow in your study of God's word.

1–2 Hours of Study a Week

If you're looking for a topical Bible study that will get you in God's Word, I've really enjoyed Cynthia Heald's studies, particularly

Becoming a Woman of Grace (Nashville, TN: Thomas Nelson, 1998); and *Becoming a Woman of Simplicity* (Colorado Springs, CO: NavPress, 2009).

Kathleen Nielson's books help you study the Bible faithfully line by line. I especially enjoyed *Proverbs: The Ways of Wisdom*, Living Word Bible Studies (Phillipsburg, NJ: P&R, 2007); and *Psalms*, vol. 1, *Songs Along the Way*, Living Word Bible Studies (Phillipsburg, NJ: P&R, 2009). She also has studies on many other books of the Bible, including John, Joshua, Colossians, and Nehemiah.

John Stott's books faithfully put you in the Bible and ask good questions. I've enjoyed his studies *The Beatitudes: Developing Spiritual Character* (Downers Grove, IL: InterVarsity Press, 1998); and *The Sermon on the Mount: 12 Studies for Individuals or Groups* (Downers Grove, IL: InterVarsity Press, 1987); but he's written many additional ones.

2–4 Hours of Study a Week

If you've ever wanted to understand how all the stories of the Bible relate to one another, Courtney Doctor's *From Garden to Glory: A Bible Study on the Bible's Story* (Lawrenceville, GA: CDM, 2016) is an excellent Bible study. Courtney takes you on a journey from Genesis to Revelation, explaining how all the smaller stories are really pointing to one larger story of redemption.

Sarah Ivill offers in-depth studies on multiple books. For an Old Testament study, try *Ezra and Nehemiah: The Good Hand of Our God Is Upon Us* (Grand Rapids, MI: Reformation Heritage, 2019).

Nancy Guthrie's Seeing Jesus in the Old Testament series (Wheaton, IL, Crossway, 2011–2014) helps you study how the Old Testament points to Jesus. She also has an excellent study on Hebrews: *Hoping for Something Better: Refusing to Settle for Life as Usual* (Carol Stream, IL: Tyndale Momentum, 2007).

Trillia Newbell's *If God Is for Us: The Everlasting Truth of Our Great Salvation* looks in-depth at one of my favorite chapters in the Bible, Romans 8 (Chicago: Moody, 2019).

Jen Wilkin has so many great studies. I enjoyed *1 Peter: A Living Hope in Christ* (Nashville, TN: Lifeway, 2016); and she also has studies on Genesis, the Sermon on the Mount, and free downloads of others at her website https://www.jenwilkin.net/downloads.

I have a Bible study on the book of Philippians called *In All Things: A Nine-Week Devotional Bible Study on Unshakeable Joy* (New York: Multnomah, 2018) as well as a Bible study for moms called *Walking with God in the Season of Motherhood: An Eleven Week Devotional Bible Study* (Colorado Springs, CO: WaterBrook, 2015).

Video Resources. If you want a free video Bible study, my husband teaches a women's Bible study at Reformed Theological Seminary that is my all-time favorite Bible study. He has a forty-two-week series on Romans and a thirty-three-week series on Hebrews. You can find them at https://www.thegospelcoalition.org/course/study-romans-kruger/#introduction; and https://rts.edu/hebrews/, respectively.

Bible Study Resources. TGC Courses is full of so many helpful Bible study tools. They have resources for every book of the Bible, as well as helpful explanations of theological doctrines. You can find them all at https://www.thegospelcoalition.org/courses/.

Seminary for Free. You can find almost every seminary course offered free at Reformed Theological Seminary by downloading the Reformed Theological Seminary mobile app.

Chapter 4: The Church: Our Home Away from Home

DeYoung, Kevin, and Ted Kluck. *Why We Love the Church.* Chicago: Moody, 2009.

Hill, Megan. *A Place to Belong: Learning to Love the Local Church.* Wheaton, IL: Crossway, 2020.

Chapter 5: It's Good News! Sharing Your Faith with Others

Packer, J. I. *Evangelism and the Sovereignty of God.* Downers Grove, IL: InterVarsity Press, 2012.

Pippert, Rebecca. *Out of the Salt Shaker and into the World: Evangelism as a Way of Life.* Downers Grove, IL: InterVarsity Press, 1979.

Chapter 6: Prayer: Pouring Out Your Heart to God

Arthur, Kay. *Lord, Teach Me to Pray in 28 Days.* Eugene, OR: Harvest, 1982.

Hill, Megan. *Praying Together: The Priority and Privilege of Prayer: In Our Homes, Communities, and Churches.* Wheaton, IL: Crossway, 2016.

Keller, Timothy. *Prayer: Experiencing Awe and Intimacy with God.* New York: Penguin, 2016.

Chapter 7: Family and Friendship: Loving Your Nearest Neighbors

Hoover, Christine. *Messy Beautiful Friendship: Finding and Nurturing Deep and Lasting Relationships.* Grand Rapids, MI: Baker, 2017.

Keller, Timothy, and Kathy Keller. *The Meaning of Marriage: Facing the Complexities of Commitment with the Wisdom of God.* New York: Penguin, 2013.

Tripp, Paul David. *What Did You Expect? Redeeming the Realities of Marriage.* Wheaton, IL: Crossway, 2010.

Chapter 8: Temptations: In the World, but Not of It

Brooks, Thomas. *Precious Remedies Against Satan's Devices.* Puritan Paperbacks. Edinburgh: Banner of Truth, 2019. First published 1652.

Chapter 9: Joy in the Journey: Cultivating Contentment in All Seasons

Hill, Megan. *Contentment: Seeing God's Goodness: 31-Day Devotionals for Life.* Phillipsburg, NJ: P&R, 2018.

Burroughs, Jeremiah. *The Rare Jewel of Christian Contentment.* Puritan Paperbacks. Edinburgh: Banner of Truth, 1964. First published 1646.

Kruger, Melissa. *The Envy of Eve: Cultivating Contentment in a Covetous World.* Fern, Scotland: Christian Focus, 2012.

Chapter 10: Service: Spending Your Life on Others

Challies, Tim. *Do More Better: A Practical Guide to Productivity.* Minneapolis: Cruciform Press, 2015.

Perman, Matt. *What's Best Next: How the Gospel Transforms the Way You Get Things Done.* Grand Rapids, MI: Zondervan, 2014.

Tozer, A. W. *The Pursuit of God.* The Project Gutenburg (2008). http://www.gutenberg.org/files/25141/25141-h/25141-h.htm.

Chapter 11: Discernment: Choosing What Is Best

Anderson, Hannah. *All That's Good: Recovering the Lost Art of Discernment.* Chicago: Moody, 2018.

Challies, Tim. *The Discipline of Spiritual Discernment.* Wheaton, IL: Crossway, 2007.

DeYoung, Kevin. *Just Do Something: A Liberating Approach to Finding God's Will.* Chicago: Moody, 2009.

Appendix 2

When Callings Clash

Submission

Submission. It's a word loaded with a powder keg of emotions. We live in a culture more accustomed to questioning authority than submitting to it. Those in leadership are often viewed with mistrust rather than respect. Many have felt the sting of poor leadership in their homes, churches, and government. For some, this word, *submission*, is associated with weakness and inability rather than strength and dignity.

However, the Bible provides us with simple and clear commands regarding submission. Wives should submit to their husbands as to the Lord (Eph. 5:22). Civilians should submit to their governing authorities (Rom. 13:1). God's people should submit to their leaders in the church (Heb. 13:17). Jesus serves as the perfect example of submission, praying on the eve of his crucifixion, "Not my will, but yours be done" (Luke 22:42).

Submission is part of the Christian life. None of us is free from authority.

While every Christian is called to submit in some form, Scripture also provides examples of when God's people disobeyed those in leadership so they could faithfully follow God's commands. Rahab failed to submit to her king when she hid the Israelite spies. She chose to align herself with the people of God and was rewarded because of her actions (Josh. 2:1–6; Heb. 11:31; James 2:25).

Abigail didn't submit to her husband's sinful injustice toward David. She secretly met David and his men in order to rightly repay them for their service. Her discernment saved her family from the disaster that was upon them (1 Sam. 25:3–42). Peter and the other apostles didn't submit to the Jewish leading council when commanded to refrain from speaking or teaching in the name of Jesus. They boldly replied, "We must obey God rather than men" (Acts 5:29).

These passages clarify that submission is not merely passive obedience to authority. It is an active and thoughtful obedience first to God and then to the authorities he has placed over us. At times, each of us will wrestle with God on how to apply the clear commands of Scripture in the complicated and gray areas of our experience.

How are we as believers to navigate the waters of submission when we find ourselves in a clash of callings? What are we to do when our obedience to God or the betterment of his people collides with the call to submit to our husband, church, or government? Two biblical principles can guide us as we seek to honor God in our submission.

Principle 1: It Is Sinful to Submit to Sinful Commands

First, we must acknowledge that we should never submit to authorities by following their leadership into sinful actions. When King Darius ordered that no one could petition any god except himself, Daniel was right to disobey the lesser command from Darius and continue his regular habit of prayer (Dan. 6). If a husband were to command a wife to stop reading the Bible or meeting with God's people, she would be right to go against his leadership in order to follow the clear teaching of Scripture (Col. 3:16; Heb. 10:25).

In the book of Acts we are told the story of Ananias and his wife, Sapphira. Ananias sold a piece of property to give to the disciples but kept back for himself some of the proceeds, with the knowledge of his wife. When Peter confronted Ananias with his sinful actions, immediately Ananias fell down and died. A few hours later when Peter asked Sapphira about the piece of property, she continued in the lie and suffered the same consequence as her husband (Acts 5:1–11).

A husband's headship doesn't mean his wife will escape judgment for her complicity in their sinful actions. When a husband, church, or government asks a Christian to sin, the believer always has the responsibility to obey God.

Principle 2: It Is Not Sinful to Influence or Persuade God-Given Authorities

An authority over us may choose a less wise course of action that is not necessarily a sinful one. Perhaps a wife truly believes that a certain schooling choice is the best option for their children or would like to attend a more biblically based church, but her husband disagrees. Perhaps a church makes what some in the congregation feel is an unwise decision on using funds. Perhaps a government makes laws that seem to promote injustice, while not necessarily causing an individual to sin. While a believer may be called to submit in these areas, it is also appropriate to respectfully engage and present one's case before his or her authority.

Following are a few principles that can guide us as we approach those in leadership with our concerns regarding their decisions.

Seek the Lord in Prayer

Before Nehemiah approached King Artaxerxes to speak with him about rebuilding the walls of Jerusalem, he went before the Lord in prayer and fasting. For four months he patiently prayed and waited before bringing the matter up to the king (Neh. 1). Prior to Esther presenting her request to her husband, she asked that

Mordecai gather all the Jews together to fast on her behalf. As we go before the authorities, we should first spend time in prayer and fasting, asking the Lord to bless our requests. It's also important to pursue wise council and support from godly people.

Choose an Appropriate Time and Place

Esther asked King Xerxes to join her for a private feast before asking him to save her people from destruction. She didn't offer her request before all his officials in court but waited until they were alone, with only Haman there to hear her request (Est. 4–5).

Each of us would be wise to consider the timing we choose to bring up areas of disagreement with those in authority. A wife might ask if she could meet her husband for lunch or dinner to discuss a specific topic. A church member would be wise to wait for a moment other than Sunday after the sermon to discuss his particular concern with his pastor. Choosing an appropriate time and location demonstrates respectful consideration of the person in authority over you.

Present Your Request with Respectful Boldness

When Nehemiah went before the king, he was "very much afraid" (Neh. 2:2). Esther also felt the weight of her request, telling Mordecai, "If I perish, I perish" (Est. 4:16). Yet both of them went before their leader with a respectful boldness that won them favor. They had the courage to ask, but they did so in a manner that honored the one of whom they made the request. As we seek to influence those in leadership over us, we can boldly put our requests before them, but we must do so in a way that demonstrates respect to the role and authority God has given them in our lives.

Submit to God's Providence

In the end, a husband may not agree to his wife's request. A church may continue down a path that seems unwise. A government may make choices that fail to promote the welfare of those it governs. In these moments we must submit, trusting in the Lord and leaning not on our own understanding. Proverbs 21:1 encourages us: "The king's heart is a stream of water in the hand of the LORD; he turns it wherever he will." Ultimately, God is providentially at work through the authorities in our lives. They are the human agents by whom God is fulfilling his good purpose for each of us (Rom. 8:28).

We are called to submit our lives first to God and, second, to those in authority over us. The way may not always be as clear as we would like, but our willingness to humbly entrust our submission to God forces us to a new and deeper understanding of his sovereign goodness. Thankfully, we follow first and foremost a Savior who knows not only the painful cost of submission, but also the joyful purposes for which God intends to use our willing obedience.

Notes

1. Susan Hunt, *Spiritual Mothering: The Titus 2 Model for Women Mentoring Women* (Wheaton, IL: Crossway, 1992).
2. S. P. W. "Call Back," *Herald of Gospel Liberty*, vol. 102 (Dayton, OH: Christian Publishing Association, 1910), 833, accessed September 27, 2019, https://books.google.com/books?id=RCAN4MNFKJYC&pg=RA5-PA1&lpg=RA5-PA1&dq=call+back+#v=onepage&q&f=false.
3. "State of the Bible 2017: Top Findings," Barna website, April 4, 2017, accessed July 31, 2019, https://www.barna.com/research/state-bible-2017-top-findings/.
4. John Flavel, "The Fountain of Life," in *Voices from the Past: Puritan Devotional Readings*, ed. Richard Rushing (Edinburgh: Banner of Truth, 2009), 5.
5. "The Word Hand," Navigators website, accessed August 1, 2019, https://www.navigators.org/resource/the-word-hand/.
6. The Bible Memory App, https://biblememory.com.
7. Verse Card Maker, http://www.mcscott.org.
8. Melissa Kruger, "My Favorite Bible in a Year Reading Plan," The Gospel Coalition website, December 29, 2015, accessed July 25, 2019, https://www.thegospelcoalition.org/blogs/melissa-kruger/my-favorite-bible-in-a-year-reading-plan-2/.
9. "Abide: Free Tools for Studying God's Word," Risen Motherhood website, accessed August 1, 2019, https://www.risenmotherhood.com/bible-study-worksheets.
10. Jackie Hill Perry, Twitter, personal post, August 2, 2018, https://twitter.com/jackiehillperry/status/1025166734981033984?lang=en.
11. If you're not attending a church, you can find a list of Bible-believing churches at The Gospel Coalition church directory. It can help you find a church in your area to visit this week. https://www.thegospelcoalition.org/churches/.
12. J. I. Packer, *Evangelism and the Sovereignty of God* (Downers Grove, IL: InterVarsity Press, 1961), 122.
13. "One-Verse Evangelism: How to Share Christ's Love Conversationally and Visually," Navigators website, accessed August 1, 2019, https://www.navigators.org/resource/one-verse-evangelism.

14. Thomas à Kempis, *The Imitation of Christ* (London: Fontana, 1963), 134.
15. Before we begin, it's important to note that physical, sexual, emotional, and spiritual abuse can happen in our closest relationships. The statistics tell a grim story. One in three female murder victims is killed by an intimate partner. One in seven women has been injured or stalked by an intimate partner. James 4:1–2 explains, "What causes quarrels and what causes fights among you? Is it not this, that your passions are at war within you? You desire and do not have, so you murder." Sinful passions can overflow into violence, even among family and close friends. The very first family experienced this painful reality (Gen. 4:1–16). Let me say clearly that if you're the victim of domestic abuse of any kind, please get help immediately. Find a mentor, friend, pastor, elder, or teacher with whom you can seek advice, support, and care. If the abuse is physical or sexual, I encourage you to also go to the police. The abuse is not your fault—you are not responsible for the harm someone else chose to inflict upon you. Seek help and know that the Lord sees all, knows all, and will one day bring justice for every wrong committed.
16. Thomas Brooks, *Precious Remedies Against Satan's Devices* (Philadelphia, Jonathan Pounder, 1810), 131.
17. Brooks, *Precious Remedies Against Satan's Devices*, 223.
18. Brooks, *Precious Remedies Against Satan's Devices*, 233.
19. Christopher Klein, "Fooling Hitler: The Elaborate Ruse behind D-Day," History website, June 3, 2014, accessed July 31, 2019, https://www.history.com/news/fooling-hitler-the-elaborate-ruse-behind-d-day.
20. See the Westminster Larger Catechism, questions 150–53.
21. Anne Dutton, cited in *Seasons of the Heart: A Year of Devotions from One Generation of Women to Another*, comp. Donna Kelderman (Grand Rapids, MI: Reformation Heritage, 2013), January 7 entry.
22. à Kempis, *The Imitation of Christ*, 136.
23. Packer, *Evangelism and the Sovereignty of God*, 86.
24. Cited in Elisabeth Elliot, *Secure in the Everlasting Arms* (Grand Rapids, MI: Baker, 2009), 136.
25. http://www.crown.org/wp-content/uploads/2017/05/Managing-Our-Finances-Bulletin-Insert.pdf. https://shop.crown.org/p-63-biblical-financial-study-collegiate-edition-student-manual-kjv.aspx.
26. https://gifts.churchgrowth.org; https://blog.lifeway.com/explorethebible/downloads/spiritual-gifts-inventory/.
27. "Resources," The Truth Project website, accessed July 31, 2019, https://truthproject.webflow.io/resources) https://uploads-ssl.webflow.com/5b86e23f49d2a07415f443d9/5bfeb24d7ffa1be32b8f3367_Gods%20Pattern%20for%20Financial%20Success%20from%20Ron%20Blue%20Institute.pdf.
28. Tim Challies, *The Discipline of Spiritual Discernment* (Wheaton, IL: Crossway, 2007), 61.

General Index

obedience: to authority, 99–100, 175–76; to God, 20, 39, 49–50, 52, 68, 97, 100, 104, 115, 132–33, 176–79; to God's word, 50, 52, 68, 90, 104, 159–60; of Jesus, 49, 175; to Jesus, 36, 50, 77

Packer, J. I., 75, 127
parenting, 26, 58, 64, 95, 99–100, 102–3
pastors, 20, 46, 57–59, 63–64, 72, 88, 175, 178
patience, 57, 96, 98–105, 111, 128, 145
Paul: contentment of, 124–30, 133–34; example of mentoring, 24, 28, 41, 47, 80, 90; instructions for mentoring, 22, 24, 31
Pentecost, 55, 133
Perry, Jackie Hill, 63
podcasts, 54, 57, 148, 156
pornography, 111
prayer: in the church, 55–56, 59, 63–64, 80, 83; evangelism and, 72–78; habit of, 32–33, 80, 83, 86, 91, 104, 163–64, 176; hindrances to, 84–87, 91; of Jesus, 24, 80, 82–90, 107; Lord's Prayer, the, 24, 82, 89–90; with mentors, 33–35, 38, 89, 91, 106, 162–64; methods of, 83–84, 87–91; relationship with God in, 62, 79–91, 161
pride, 58, 83, 96, 98, 109, 115, 128, 159
Priscilla, 158
Pusey, E. B., 134

Reformed Theological Seminary, 81
Risen Motherhood, 51

Satan, 23, 42, 107, 109, 112–19, 161
Saving Private Ryan, 107–8
self-care, 43
self-centeredness, 21, 62, 94–95, 101–2, 143
self-control, 22, 32, 57, 59, 104, 111
self-denial, 64, 128, 147
self-fulfillment, 143

self-glory, 109
service: in the church, 37, 54, 57–59, 61–65, 141–49, 161; mentoring and, 21–26, 32–33; prayer and, 85–86; for others, 32, 95–97, 114, 128, 137–49
sexual immorality, 96, 111, 159–60, 182n15
shepherds. *See* pastors
Simmons, Ruth Chou, 137
sin: in the church, 63, 76, 177; confessing, 34, 87, 102, 104, 112, 119; effect on relationships, 95–106, 122; freedom from, 36, 37, 69–71, 73–74, 137; forgiveness of, 44, 49, 69–71, 98–99, 112, 117; of leaders, 63, 176–78; patterns of, 37, 58, 111–19, 133; sharing about, 29, 33–34, 36, 37; struggle with, 36, 37, 42, 87, 101–6, 109–19
slander, 22, 31–32, 96
social media, 43, 46, 63, 128, 140, 158
spiritual gifts, 37, 138–39
spiritual mentoring. *See* mentoring
spiritual mothering. *See* mentoring
submission: to authority, 58, 100, 105, 175–79; to God, 39, 100, 105, 113, 159, 175–79; of Jesus, 175; of wives, 22, 99–100, 103, 175–76; suffering, 44, 63, 70, 96, 126–30, 138–39, 146. *See also* trials

temptation: from the devil, 109, 112–17, 119; from the flesh, 36, 101, 109–12, 117, 119; God's word and, 42, 51, 58, 109–19, 161; prayer and, 118–19, 129–30, 134; relationships and, 99–102; resisting, 107, 117–19, 132, 161, 163; from the world, 22, 109–10, 117, 119, 145, 152, 161
Team Ministry, 147
Ten Commandments, the, 25, 94–95
The Gospel Coalition, 51, 100, 105
The Truth Project, 148

Scripture Index

THE GOSPEL **COALITION**

The Gospel Coalition is a fellowship of evangelical churches deeply committed to renewing our faith in the gospel of Christ and to reforming our ministry practices to conform fully to the Scriptures. We have committed ourselves to invigorating churches with new hope and compelling joy based on the promises received by grace alone through faith alone in Christ alone.

We desire to champion the gospel with clarity, compassion, courage, and joy—gladly linking hearts with fellow believers across denominational, ethnic, and class lines. We yearn to work with all who, in addition to embracing our confession and theological vision for ministry, seek the lordship of Christ over the whole of life with unabashed hope in the power of the Holy Spirit to transform individuals, communities, and cultures.

Through its women's initiatives, The Gospel Coalition aims to support the growth of women in faithfully studying and sharing the Scriptures; in actively loving and serving the church; and in spreading the gospel of Jesus Christ in all their callings.

Join the cause and visit TGC.org for fresh resources that will equip you to love God with all your heart, soul, mind, and strength, and to love your neighbor as yourself.

TGC.org

Also Available from the Gospel Coalition

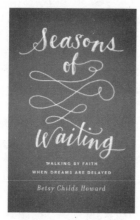

For more information, visit **crossway.org**.